Page 1
*Scene from the Formula 750 brigade, Brands Hatch, April 1971. Left to right: Peter Williams, Charlie Sanby, Paul Smart, Percy Tait, Brian Kemp, Geoff Barry and Ray Petty*

Page 2
*Jack Brett airborne on the classic Manx Norton*

Left
*Oliver's Mount circuit, Scarborough, September 1947*

Cover
*Don Morley's camera caught John Surtees in action on a 1000 cc Vincent for the front cover, and Bob Lomas on a KTT Velocette for the back cover*

Published in 1990 by Osprey Publishing
59 Grosvenor Street, London W1X 9DA

British Library Cataloguing in Publication Data

Walker, Mick
    Classic British racing motorcycles.
    1. British racing motorcycles, history
    I. Title
    629.2275
ISBN 0-85045-880-3

Editor Ian Penberthy
Designer Alex Charles

Printed by BAS Printers Limited
Over Wallop, Hampshire
Great Britain

*When British bikes ruled the world. Photograph
shows, left to right: C. Nebitt, R. Schroeder
(Velocettes) and the future Norton works star Ray
Amm ('Garden Gate' Manx) at South Africa's
premier road race, the Port Elizabeth 200, 10 January
1950*

# Contents

# About the author

Mick Walker is an enthusiast for all forms of motor-cycle sport. He has been a successful competitor and has helped many to triumph with his profound knowledge of tuning. There is virtually no aspect of the business in which Mick has not been active at some point, and that includes being an importer of exotic Italian race-bred machines. Today, he heads a thriving company that specializes in the supply of spare parts to Ducati owners and racers around the world.

Mick rode a variety of racers during the classic era, including an AJS 7R, Manx Norton, Greeves Silverstone, a brace of BSA Gold Stars, various Ducatis and even 50 and 125 cc Hondas.

Above
*The author (right) with rider Derek Ward, Cadwell Park, 1969. The bike is the super-quick, Walker-tuned Formula Triumph Cub*

Right
*The author is no stranger to British racing motorcycles of the classic variety. He is pictured here on a 499 cc BSA Gold Star at a Snetterton national meeting in 1967*

# Introduction

Today, with Japanese motorcycles generally dominating on both road and track, it is perhaps difficult to appreciate that the situation was not always so. Once there was a time when virtually every manufacturer in Europe listed a racing machine in his catalogue and every firm was anxious for the publicity resulting from success in a major event. For a long time British machines dominated the scene. In the years between the two world wars, Nortons, Rudges, Sunbeams, AJSs and Velocettes shared the spoils of victory despite the efforts of manufacturers in Italy, Germany, Sweden, France and Belgium. It was not until the mid 1930s that success began to come the way of the continentals, firstly in the Lightweight class. Racegoers began to see Guzzi and Benelli from Italy in the list of winners, along with Germany's DKW.

Britons were able to console themselves that they still dominated in the 350 and 500 cc classes, and these were after all the most important races. But just prior to the outbreak of war Germany's 350 DKW and supercharged 500 BMW twin began to score, whilst the Italian Gilera four was a challenger to the BMW in the bigger class. In 1939 Georg Meier won the Senior TT on a BMW, and Dorino Serafina the Ulster GP on a Gilera. Ironically, Britain's leading marque, Norton, had decided earlier that year to concentrate on the production of motorcycles for less sporting battles ahead.

After the conflict Germany's industry lay in ruins and British AJS, Norton and Velocette machinery once again dominated, at least in the bigger classes. In 1947, after seven years' absence, the TT once more became *the* annual fixture for racing enthusiasts and although Guzzi won the Lightweight, British Velocette and Norton machines took the Junior and

Senior events. Another facet of the immediate post-war period was the ban on supercharging, and the use of low octane 'pool' petrol.

The World Championship series was first run in 1949. Mondial and Guzzi dominated the Lightweight classes, while British machines were dominant in the 350 cc (Frith, Velocette), 500 cc (Graham, AJS) and Sidecar (Oliver/Jenkinson, Norton).

Even though Gilera were the 1950 500 cc World Champions, generally British machines continued to control the larger solo classes until the end of 1952. By then the Italian Gilera and MV Agusta fours and Guzzi singles were obviously quicker, but the British factories still had the best riders. But with several top liners, including Geoff Duke, joining the Italian companies for 1953, the tide was about to turn, unfortunately, forever. From then on it was only on the Isle of Man and to a lesser extent in Ulster that the British singles were to overcome the Italians, and then thanks in no small part to the brilliant riding of the Rhodesian Norton star, Ray Amm.

Meanwhile, the world sidecar title had been the preserve of the almost unbeatable Eric Oliver from 1949 to 1953 inclusive (except for 1952 when Cyril Smith was champion); but from 1954 onwards there was to be an unbroken string of successes by the German BMWs for many years—the days of the Norton singles at world level were over.

Even so, in both the solo and three-wheel events British bikes were to play a vital role at club, national and international level, as this book will reveal.

For many years after her decline as a force in world motorcycle manufacturing, Britain (and the Commonwealth) continued to provide the very best riders, men such as Surtees, Hocking, Hailwood, Read and Sheene, to name but a few.

In the course of compiling this particular title I was fortunate enough to come into contact with a myriad of people who were able to help in some way.

Almost all were only too kind and gladly provided whatever help they could. Unfortunately, the list is almost endless but even if your name is not mentioned below I shall be eternally grateful for the help I received.

So I offer acknowledgements to the following, in no particular order of merit: Dan Shorey, John Surtees, the late Steve Lancefield, Mike Cutler, Ken Kavanagh, Reg Everett, Dave Croxford, Tom Mortimer, John Kirkby, Eric Kirk, Paul Smart, Brian Woolley, Peter Dobson, Peter Williams, Doug Jackson, Hugh Anderson and Barry Hickmott. The last for helping so much with the two-stroke chapter.

Photographs came from a variety of sources including Len Thorpe, Phillip Tooth, Ronald Hunt, George Nutall, Ken Kavanagh, Tom Mortimer, Reg Everett, Doug Jackson, Barry Hickmott, Mike Cutler, the late George Brown, Fritz Egli, Alan Kirk, Richard Walker and my old friends at the EMAP archives, now in the hands of the ever-helpful Kim White. Cover photography is the work of Don Morley.

I would also like to acknowledge the patience of my long-suffering wife Susan, and the efforts of my secretary Carol Green in typing the manuscript.

Last but not least to the super-efficient Osprey editorial team of Helen Dawson and editor Ian Penberthy, not forgetting former editor Tony Thacker who encouraged my original idea.

*Classic British Racing Motorcycles* is intended as the first of a new series looking at the major players throughout the world who produced racing machines during the 'classic' period. All that is left is to hope that you gain as much enjoyment reading the finished product as I have had in compiling it.

Mick Walker
Wisbech, Cambridgeshire
September 1989

# 1
# AJS 7R—the boy racer

An 'Ajay' competed in the TT as early as 1911, when a pair of 350s finished 15th and 16th in the Junior race. This was some two years after AJS (Albert John Stevens) began trading as a limited company in Wolverhampton in 1909.

Having won their first TT, the Junior, in 1914 the firm returned to the racing scene after the Great War to become outstandingly successful in the 350 cc class at home and on the Continent. The marque won three Junior TTs in succession in 1920/ 1921/1922, and in 1921 Howard Davies, riding a 350 ohv AJS, became the first rider to win a Senior TT on a Junior machine, a feat which has never been repeated. It was also on AJS machinery that Jimmy Simpson created the first Isle of Man lap records at over 60 and 70 mph in 1924 and 1926 respectively.

With motorcycle racing becoming ever more competitive in the late 1920s the Wolverhampton company developed new overhead-camshaft works models for the 1927 season. The single camshaft was chain driven and featured a double gear oil pump and dry sump, which replaced the earlier AJS lubrication system of a primitive foot-operated pump and total loss method. There were both 350 and 500 cc versions. An unusual feature of the design was the foot operation for *both* brakes, the theory being that this left the right hand free to operate the throttle and gearchange lever.

*First public appearance of the 7R, with AMC's sales director Jack West, was at Brands Hatch when it was still a grass circuit, 14 March 1948*

**Above**
*Australian Ernie Ring with his 349 cc AJS at Boreham in late April 1952. He missed victory by less than a wheel's length from John Storr (Norton)*

**Below**
*Factory-fresh 7R, circa 1953*

*7Rs in action at Crystal Palace, 18 June 1955. On the left is future AMC and Suzuki star Frank Perris*

But although the new 'cammy' engines proved reliable they were too slow, the larger machine in particular. To allow extra development of the camshaft engines, the company reverted to its pushrod design for 1928 and with it gained a fair amount of success abroad.

In 1929, AJS re-introduced the ohc engine with some small but significant improvements, plus a number of changes to the running gear, including stronger forks and larger diameter brakes. As proof of its success with the redesign, at least of the 350, the company had a second place in the Junior TT, and victory in the Grands Prix of Austria, Germany and Ulster.

The following year, 1930, saw the introduction of the R7 'over-the-counter' racer—the forerunner of its much more famous son, the post-war 7R 'Boy Racer'. But although the R7 proved popular with private owners, it never did achieve the success of its rivals, the KTT Velocette and ohc Norton.

At works level the company could rejoice in Jimmy Guthrie's 1930 Lightweight TT victory, but this was to be the last taste of success before a bout of financial problems caused by the worldwide economic depression threatened the future of the whole company. By mid 1931, the Stevens empire was on the rocks, and the factory doors closed.

But this was not to be the end of the road for AJS, as it was acquired by the Collier brothers, for their Matchless business in south-east London. The Colliers had the foresight to keep the AJS and Matchless marques as separate entities—at least, during the all-important early days of the new venture.

At first the move to London, and of course the Depression, caused a great reduction in the AJS racing effort. But by 1934 the marque once again re-entered racing at international level. In the 350 cc class the engine remained basically the same Stevens inspired chain-driven ohc unit, but saw a gradual improvement in specification—for example, aluminium bronze heads in 1934, a bi-metal head with bronze skull in 1935, and an aluminium alloy component with screwed-in valve seats for 1937.

Aluminium alloys were used extensively for the cycle parts, whilst magnesium was employed for both gearbox and engine castings. This meant that weight could be kept in check—the 1935 works 350 single weighed only 270 lb, although in 1938, when rear suspension was added, it climbed to over the 300 lb mark. The suspension was by an unusual pivoted-fork which attached to plunger spring boxes at the rear of the frame. Another notable improvement was the large alloy front brake. Nearly all these improvements were adopted on the R7 model which continued to be produced in small batches for private owners.

At the same time the Matt Wright-designed, supercharged, 50-degree, watercooled 500 four arrived on the scene. But although it was super quick—the first 100 mph lap in a classic race in the 1939 Ulster GP, for example—it was fragile and its handling far from perfect.

Then war broke out and racing came to a halt for six long years.

After the conflict supercharging was banned which ended the career of the V4 and rather stunted

the new E90 Porcupine twin (see Chapter 6). The Porcupine made its debut in 1947, and the following February AJS announced that they had a 350 model to back up the newly launched 500 twin, but in this instance it was also to be offered for sale to the private customer.

Compared to the pre-war R7 the new machine, designated 7R, shared very little except its cubic capacity and the use of a single overhead camshaft driven by a Weller-tensioned chain. As for the frame, this was largely a copy of the works E90 Porcupine, of wide-spaced double cradle design in

*AMC depot during the 1955 Manx Grand Prix practice—R. Mason and F. W. Neil*

*The great Bob McIntyre in vivid action at Stowe Corner, Silverstone, 18 April 1959. He was fourth in the 350 cc Championship race after holding second until his engine went off song. The race was won by MV-mounted John Surtees*

welded steel tube. The front forks were modified AMC teledraulics, while at the rear the swinging arm was controlled by a pair of oil-damped spring units. In the braking department conical hubs were used, the front featuring two leading-shoe operation.

But the centre of attraction was the totally new 74 × 81 mm 348 cc single-cylinder power unit. To keep weight to a minimum, wide use was made of magnesium castings and these were finished in a highly distinctive gold-coloured, corrosion-inhibiting paint.

The engine warrants a detailed description because not only was it to remain in production for some 15 years but an enlarged version, the Matchless G50, appeared in 1958. Later still the Seeley G50 continued the theme and is today considered the premier engine for the all-important Senior class at classic events around the world.

The aluminium alloy cylinder barrel had a shrunk-in iron liner and was held in position by four long bolts which passed from the crankcase right through to the cylinder head.

A forged piston was employed, together with a massive I-section steel con-rod, the latter featuring a bushed small-end and a duralumin caged single row big-end. There were circumferential webs to the eyes of the big- and small-ends to provide additional strength.

The solid steel crankshaft flywheels were drilled and recessed on their inner faces to accommodate the big-end bearing, thus keeping the lateral width of the assembly to a minimum. The crankpin, following normal company practice, consisted of a toughened alloy-steel pin on which a hardened race was pressed.

The timing-side mainshaft had a single large-diameter journal ball-race while on the drive side there was, first, a double-caged roller-bearing and then on the outside a further single roller-bearing. At the extremity of the shaft came a conventional cam-type shock absorber.

The magnesium crankcase had strengthening

webs, arranged in such a manner as to best withstand the stress of racing use.

The timing cover encased the gear-type oil pumps, both of which had cylindrical bodies. Each pump took its drive co-axially from a pinion in the timing gear train, the delivery pump being driven from the magneto-drive idler pinion and the scavenging pump from the main half-time wheel. There were only two external pipes which were short ones running between the oil tank and the pumps. The main feed from the delivery pump went directly to the big-end; another feed went, by way of a pipe cast integrally with the magnesium alloy chaincase straight to the overhead camshaft which was drilled so that oil was led to the lift faces of the cams. The single crankcase breather valve was located in the drilled drive-side mainshaft and exited on to the primary chain.

The timing case featured a small cover plate, which provided access to the magneto-drive pinion. The timing of the strap-mounted racing Lucas magneto had a vernier adjustment produced by an AJS method of using a pegged locking washer and a pinion boss, each of which had a different number of radially disposed drillings with which the pegs mated. This same type of adjustment was also used for the camshaft.

The massive, but at the same time light, aluminium alloy cylinder head casting had unusual finning. Round the centrally disposed exhaust port the horizontal fins extended until they reached their maximum depth between the port and the ohc chaincase.

Right
*Mike Hailwood pushes his 7R into life at the start of the 1961 Junior TT. After looking set for victory, however, he was finally put out by engine trouble with just 12 miles to go.*

Below
*A 1960 version of the world famous 'Boy Racer'*

**Above**
*Rhodesian star Bruce Beale negotiating Club Corner at Westmead during the 1962 Natal 100 race*

**Below**
*Roy Mayhew guns his 7R at Snetterton on Easter Sunday 1962, when he was runner-up to Mike Hailwood and MV in both 350 and 500 cc races*

*Tom Kirby's Hornchurch workshops, with rider Roger Hunter holding the tank and mechanic Tony Goody with clutch*

Then they were squeezed in to accommodate this before swelling out again. Beneath the one piece rocker-box casting there was vertical finning, running diagonally at an angle of 45 degrees from the drive-side to the rear of the chaincase on the timing side. Both the rocker-box and camshaft housing were in magnesium.

It was possible to remove the rocker-box without first having to take the engine out of the frame *or* risking the problem of stripped threads. This was just one example of why the AMC sohc design was so much easier for the private owner to maintain than the equivalent double-knocker Manx Norton.

The camshaft ran on twin ball-races and at its 'free' end there was provision for the tacho drive.

The rockers, of toughened alloy-steel with deposited hard-metal bearing pads, were short to keep reciprocating weight to a minimum, and the rocker spindles, which ran in plain bushes, were mounted eccentrically, affording a means of setting valve clearances without recourse to screwed adjusters or shims. Incidentally, these clearances could be checked *without* disturbing the valve-spring covers.

There were, in fact, no end caps to the valves, which received the same treatment as the rockers and had a chemically deposited surface of bearing metal on their ends. Fully enclosed (another advantage over the Norton design) hairpin springs were used, these being retained by circlip type collets.

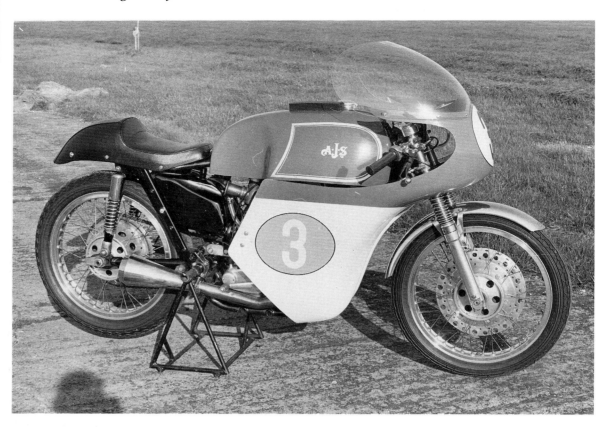

Above
*Colin Seeley took over the production rights of the 7R from AMC in 1966. Photograph shows a Seeley 350 during TT practice 1967*

Above left
*Kirby 7R, summer 1965. Many of Britain's top stars rode 'Uncle Tom's' bikes, including Mike Hailwood, Phil Read and Bill Ivy*

Left
*The Keeler 500 cc special, October 1966. Essentially, this experimental machine used a pair of sleeved 7R cylinders and heads*

The valves were set in the cylinder head at an inclusive angle of 80 degrees and the inlet port was not only downdraught but offset.

A feature of the 7R engine was its clean lines and air of robustness. In the past its appearance has generally been ascribed to the long-serving Philip Walker, who was then chief designer at AMC, but there is no doubt that racer and AMC sales director Jock West had a lot of influence in its creation. In fact, it was he who convinced the AMC board to authorize the project, even though Walker carried out the actual design and it was West who gave the 7R its first public outing, when he created a stir by making an appearance with the new bike at Brands Hatch on Sunday 14 March 1948.

By then the prototype had already covered several hundred miles on the King's highway. Brands Hatch in those days was still a grass circuit, however, this didn't stop the intrepid West from doing a 'hands-off' at full bore to prove the stability of the newcomer. The large crowd went home suitably impressed to spread the word.

Some 77 examples were produced in the first year, with one particular event undoubtedly being the highlight. This was Geoff Murdoch's inspired ride to annex fourth spot in the 1948 Senior TT on his Junior AJS, a truly outstanding achievement. Backing this up was Maurice Cann's fifth in the Junior TT and Phil Heath's second in the Junior Manx GP.

This set the Plumstead single off to a flying start, and it was to record countless wins in every type of event including grands prix and the Manx, but never strangely a TT. The nearest probably coming in the 1961 Junior when the great Mike Hailwood led the race until a gudgeon pin broke a mere 12 miles from the finish on the last lap.

As for development, the first batch of 7Rs offered 29 bhp at 6800 rpm (on pool petrol of course!), and for the first two years, apart from copper-plating the cams to counteract a rate of wear that was high on some units, engine modifications were nil. But in 1950 the flywheels were lightened, a sump fitted to the crankcase, both valves increased in diameter, the valve timing altered and roller rockers substituted for slipper type.

Two more seasons passed without further change, then in 1953 came a whole crop. Included in this batch were a shallower combustion chamber, a sodium-cooled exhaust valve, a change in inlet valve angle and diameter, modified rockers and rocker lubrication, replacement of the plain camshaft bush by a roller bearing, improved main bearings, a narrower chain for greater rigidity of the flywheel assembly, a redesigned breather and the deletion of the exterior crankcase ribs.

Status quo was again maintained throughout 1954 and 1955, while chief 1956 development was a revision in the bore and stroke measurements to 75.5 × 78 mm giving a new capacity of 349 cc. At the same time, a double timing-side main bearing and a rotating-magnet magneto were adopted. Finally, a modification was made to the inlet port shape. This mini-redesign was the work of Jack Williams who had joined AMC in 1954.

In 1957 the output was raised to 37.5 bhp and for 1958 a new camshaft, inlet port and engine breather appeared, together with a racing version of the already established AMC gearbox. This replaced the earlier Burman unit.

In 1959 engine modifications produced an additional $1\frac{1}{2}$ bhp, these included inlet port changes (again!) to improve volumetric efficiency and the use of a larger bore $1\frac{3}{8}$ in. carburettor.

For 1960 engine alterations saw closer adjustment to the vernier ignition timing, a stronger magneto strap, and more rigid float chamber mounting brackets.

The final round of annual modifications came in 1961 when the timing chest was altered to allow an improved curve for the exhaust pipe, larger gearbox mainshaft sprocket and an increase in compression ratio from 11.7 to 12:1 with a modified piston.

The cycle parts and running gear, too, were the subject of continual revision, without ever really stepping out of line with the original 7R concept. Notably over the period 1953–5, frontal area was diminished and handling improved by lowering the frame and narrowing it and the tanks; in the same era, leading- and trailing-shoes were adopted for the rear brake instead of 2LS. Later, the wheelbase was shortened and the frame further lowered in the search for improved penetration.

The final year of production was 1962, but in practice very few 7Rs were manufactured that year. As related in Chapter 4, when Colin Seeley took over the remains of the AMC 7R/G50 tooling and spares in the mid 1960s he concentrated his efforts on the larger engine. However, unlike the Manx Norton business which he also inherited, a small number of 7R-engined Seeley machines were built, although this is unlikely to have been more than half a dozen.

Total number of 7Rs built between 1948 and 1962, including the few Seeley bikes, was around 700 units.

To many enthusiasts the AJS 7R 'Boy Racer' was unquestionably the *prettiest* racing motorcycle money could buy, and today they are highly prized by their lucky owners.

# 2
# Gold Star—café racer supreme

Few motorcycles can be everything to everyone but the BSA Gold Star—the Goldie—came closer than most, A 100 mph lap at Brooklands, clubman's racing, scrambling, trials, street bike . . . the legendary Goldie could cope with almost anything.

Its origin goes back to 1937 when on the final day of June the famous TT rider Wal Handley won a Brooklands Gold Star for lapping at over 100 mph on a 500 cc iron-engined BSA Empire Star specially prepared by tuners Jack Amott and Len Crisp to run on dope. In fact, Handley's race-winning average speed was 102.27 mph, with a best lap of 105.57 mph on the Surrey banking. This outstanding performance resulted in the Empire Star title being dropped in favour of the Gold Star for the 1938 model year.

Three versions were offered: standard, competition and pure racing. Light alloy was used for the barrel and head with screw-in valve seats and the pushrod tower was an integral part of the castings. An Amal TT carb was standardized and, most surprising of all, the gearbox shell was cast in magnesium alloy. For the following year the gearbox shell reverted to aluminium but there was the advantage of an optional close-ratio cluster.

The 1939 Goldie was the last for nine years. The war meant that the production requirement was for the side-valve M20 military models rather than the expensive limited run sportster—however good. After the war the factory concentrated on the 'cooking' B31 and B33 models which were then fitted with telescopic forks. A competition model, the B32, fitted with an iron engine was offered for trials.

The next development in the Gold Star story came in 1948 when high performance versions of the B31/33 range were offered rather than direct descendants of the pre-war M24. The 350 model had an alloy barrel and head known as the ZB32, these engines were long stroke with internal dimensions of 71 × 88 mm. At this stage a 500 version was at least planned but it is doubtful if any were actually built until later.

This was designated B34 and based on the 350 but with an 85 mm bore.

The full 500 was in production by 1950 with a power output of 33 bhp, the smaller engine's power was up to 25 bhp by this time. It should be remembered that this was in the days of pool petrol which had a very low octane rating. The chassis had also received attention to keep it in line with the extra power and now featured plunger rear suspension and more stopping power thanks to a new 8 in. front brake.

The 350s, in particular, had become not only successful in off-road sport but in clubman's racing too; the Clubman's TT was organized to allow machines such as the Gold Star a chance of Isle of Man honours. With supercharging banned by the FIM, production class racing was another option open to

*Ken James with his plunger-framed, BB32 348 cc Gold Star at Goodwood, April 1951, where he won the ten-lap scratch race for clubmen.*

the Goldie. Strangely, the bike proved too successful for its own good, winning the Clubman's TT every year from 1949 to 1957 when the race was finally dropped. The Goldie domination probably killed off the appeal of the race for many people as it had become just another procession of identical machines rather similar to the Yamaha twin domination of the 1970s.

Meanwhile, the BSA works scrambles and trials teams were also proving almost unbeatable. All this success proved beneficial to the sales of the Gold Star models and to a lesser extent the mass production B31/33 range.

The engines had detailed changes for 1951 including die-cast head and barrel and bolt-on rocker boxes. The following year saw the BB32 with plunger suspension but most important were the mechanical changes. Valve angles were changed from 37 to 33 degrees and both inlet and exhaust valve diameters increased and their ports opened up to match. To take advantage of this, a larger Amal TT9 carburettor was fitted. A test of the new BB32 in *Motor Cycling* found the top speed to be 98 mph and commented: 'The engine appeared to have no vices at all, beautifully smooth, it ran cleanly up from about 4300 rpm to over 7000 rpm'.

When the 1953 model range was announced, BSA

*Tasmanian rider Peter Thurley with the CB34 on which he dominated the 1955 State Speed Championships. This included standing-start and flying speed records—the latter at over 125 mph—and winning the 750 and 1000 solo events*

*J. J. Wood (Duke BSA), winner of the 1955 North West 200 350 cc scratch race*

*Double Clubman's TT winner in 1956, Bernard Codd, seen here on his Senior mount*

revealed that the Gold Star models were to be considerably revised. Under the B prefix, the new Goldies featured duplex cradle frames with swing-arm suspension. One year later the CB arrived, distinguishable by its massive engine finning. This motor had a shorter con-rod and oval flywheel to clear the piston. Valve adjustment was carried out by an eccentric rocker spindle to cut down on reciprocating weight and an Amal GP was specified for the first time. Power was increased to 30 bhp at 6800 rpm on the 350 and the 500 kicked out 37 bhp at 6600 rpm. Other changes included a timed engine breather, EN36 crankpin and Nimonic 80 exhaust valve, and finally the Clubman version of both the 350 and 500 had clip-ons as standard equipment. The basic formula for the café racer of the 1960s had arrived.

Under revised ACU regulations for the Clubman's TT, machines had to be equipped with lighting sets, speedometer and an efficient(!) silencer. The new DB Gold Star for 1955 utilized a standard Lucas Magdyno and battery, a 6½ in. Lucas headlight with separate lens and reflector, and the tubular silencer was filled with glass wool. This silencer was not the type currently associated with the Clubman's Goldie but more like the standard item of the time made by Burgess.

Virtually the last stage of development came in 1956 with the introduction of a 190 mm front brake and a 1½ in. GP carburettor for the 500 which pumped out 42 bhp at 7000 rpm. That year also saw a double Clubman's TT win when Lincolnshire's Bernard Codd took a brace of Gold Stars to victory. Codd's average speed on the larger bike was 86.33 mph whilst he averaged 82.02 mph on the 350. The following year the 350 was dropped but track success came in the form of a win at Daytona in the 100-miler and at Thruxton in the 500 endurance race.

From then on development stagnated, although former Army Captain Eddie Dow developed a 500 Goldie which with 52 bhp at 10,000 rpm promised much but actually delivered very little. More successful were the sleeved down 250 models, notably the GMS (Geoff Monty Special), which put up a string of impressive performances before the arrival of a new breed of two-strokes headed by the Greeves

Silverstone. Even though it was largely unsuccessful, the Dow BSA did lead to the development of a number of go-faster goodies for the Gold Star street rider. Coffee-bar cowboys were offered such items as the famed Taylor Dow fork conversion, Lyta polished alloy tank and even smaller components like finned rocker covers, which were sold via Eddie Dow's emporium known as 'Britain's Gold Star Shop' in Banbury, Oxfordshire, once the former Captain Dow donned his civvies.

With a maximum of 70 mph in first from its RRT2 close-ratio box, the Gold Star became the ultimate street racer. Clip-ons, swept-back exhaust, 'twittering' silencer and its aggressive look all gave the image of a performance which other roadsters of the day just couldn't match. And the poor handling of many of its twin-cylinder rivals—notably the Triumph twin—helped.

But from personal experience of riding various Gold Stars on road and track during that classic era I can explode a few myths. For a start, against real racers like the Manx Norton and AJS 7R the BSA

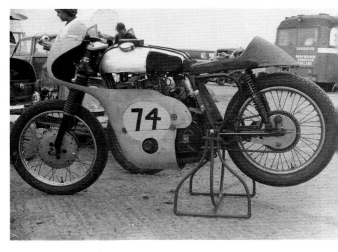

*A typical race-knitted Gold Star, Snetterton 1964. Many were converted into racers to give their owners the first taste of competitive riding*

*Eddie Dow (right) and mechanic Bert Poole examine the new Taylor Dow Special, March 1959*

*Derek Minter was one of many famous riders who began their racing careers on Gold Stars. Derek is shown here at Brands Hatch in 1956 on his 499 cc model*

just wasn't good enough, but of the two the 350 was the best. It was much more reliable, relatively smoother and more powerful for its size, and its slower speed meant that the handling and braking weren't so exposed. On the 500, certainly in DBD form, it vibrated (I experienced sheared flywheels and broken con-rods) and the handling and braking showed up badly against the pukka racers. In fact, without the Taylor Dow fork kit the handling was poor under racing conditions.

The street didn't suit the 500 Goldie much better, its high first gear making it a pain in traffic and vibration not helping matters on longer trips. But for all that the bike which is remembered today is the DBD34 Clubmans, one of a very few British bikes of the post-war period to achieve cult status. Today this is reflected by the high prices sought and obtained for really immaculate and original examples. Watch out if you are considering buying a 'Goldie' as it is a long time since 1962 when the last bikes were built and there is plenty of rubbish about to catch the unwary.

For all its faults, a good Gold Star is still an exhilarating machine to ride and more than any other it gives a true taste of the classic café racer . . . but as a *real* racer you will soon realize its limitations. A Goldie's only top six placing in a world championship race was in 1954, when the New Zealander Barry Stormont finished fifth in the 350 cc French Grand Prix at Rheims. Instead, its epitaph is that it acted as the stepping-stone for countless riders in their all-important first few outings during their racing career.

# 3
# Manx Norton—
# the professionals' choice

In 1869, James Lansdowne Norton was born, a true son of the industrial heartland of Britain, the city of Birmingham. During his life he was destined to play a vital role in the creation of an entirely new industry—that of the motorcycle. And as the influential journal *Motor Cycling* stated back in 1957; 'It can truly be said that the contributions he made to the design and construction of the motorcycle during the first quarter of the present century were of more importance than those from any other single source'. When he died in the spring of 1925 he was not only

*Artie Bell crossing the line to win the 1948 Senior TT at an average speed of 84.97 mph*

mourned wherever motorcycles were ridden as 'The Father of the Industry', but the company bearing his name went on to become a legend, and one of the very, very few names which even non-motorcyclists are able to instantly recognize.

And no one type was more responsible than the world famous overhead-camshaft racing singles—nowadays more commonly referred to under the 'Manx' title, these machines could trace their origins to the CS1 (Cam Shaft One) which was introduced in 1927. The then new cammy Norton got off to a winning start when factory rider Alec Bennett won the Senior TT at a record speed of 68.4 mph, with another CS1 rider Stanley Woods setting a record

*Geoff Duke about to push his factory Norton into life at the start of the 1950 Junior TT, in which he finished second behind team-mate Artie Bell*

lap of 70.90 mph. Shortly after this the designer of the CS1, Walter Moore, left Norton to take up the post of chief designer with NSU—and the German company promptly proceeded to build a design so similar that many observers said that NSU stood for Norton Spares Used!

As it happened all this didn't matter too much as Norton were able to introduce a major redesign in 1930. This was the work of the gifted Arthur Carroll. Carroll's engine was virtually brand new, retaining only the traditional 490 cc long-stroke measurements of 79 × 100 mm. There was also a 348 cc (71 × 88 mm) version.

Moore's splined vertical shaft was replaced by one incorporating a floating centre with Oldhams couplings. The raised area of the lower bevel housing was gone, but the clean lines of the timing-case on the CS1, with its reciprocating oil pump, were swel-

led by a machined housing for the new circular gear pump, with internally a layout for the drives to both the pump and the magneto very similar to that used on the 350 ohc Velocette KTT. The Moore cambox, which could be made oil tight, was scrapped and in its place one where, for adjustment, straight rockers protruded at their outer ends through slots in the box, which was forever after a constant source of leaking lubricant. As most racing buffs will know, even the final Manx models produced almost 50 years on still suffered in this fashion, the partial cure being to lag the cambox area with foam to soak up the excess oil.

Strangely, the new Norton was beaten into third place in the 1930 Senior TT—by the four-valve Rudges of Walter Handley and Graham Walker. But after this the cammy Norton effort got into top gear as development made it faster each year.

From 1929 the Norton racing team manager (and development engineer) had been Joe Craig, who had raced Nortons himself with considerable success during much of the 1920s, including several vic-

*Lovely period shot of New Zealander Rod Coleman arriving with his brand-new Manx for the 1951 TT*

*Denis Parkinson, winner of the Scottish Speed Championships at St Andrews, 23 July 1949*

tories in his native Ulster. But it was really during the period from 1931 onwards that the Carroll engine with Craig as race chief, and riders of the calibre of Jimmy Simpson, 'Crasher' White, Tim Hunt, Stanley Woods, Jimmy Guthrie, Freddie Frith and Harold Daniell, was to make the Norton team world famous.

From 1931 the works bikes introduced down-

draught carbs, four-speed gearboxes and 14 mm spark plugs. And it was in this state of tune that Tim Hunt scored a sensational 350/500 TT double; the Senior race at a record average of 77.90 mph,

*Geoff Duke's factory Norton for the 1952 Junior TT*

with fellow Norton rider Jimmy Simpson setting the first over 80 mph lap at 80.82 mph.

In 1932 the first International model was introduced for sale to private customers who wished to go racing. But it should be remembered that it was also used for a variety of other tasks including the International Six Days Trial—hence its name.

Racing at works level saw Stanley Woods score another TT double in 1932 and 1933, when he took the average speed to over 80 mph for the first time—to 81.04 mph. By then, increases in power had meant that Norton had replaced the cast-iron cylinder head with a bronze component—and fitted hairpin valve springs for the first time. The head material changed once again in 1933 to a bronze skull with aluminium fins. The cylinder was also bi-metal.

The Scot Jimmy Guthrie scored yet another TT double in 1934 when the works machines were fitted with megaphones and twin spark ignition for the first time.

But when Stanley Woods left to join the Swedish Husqvarna concern observers wondered if this would affect Norton's fortunes—but it didn't.

Then Woods joined the Italian Guzzi team, and mounted on one of the new V-twins he finally beat the Nortons—although the gap was a mere four seconds at the finish of the 1935 Senior TT, with Woods taking victory at 84.68 mph from Jimmy Guthrie. But Guthrie and Norton got their revenge by winning the Ulster GP the same year at 90.98 mph

*Duke (seated) being congratulated by Norton's managing director, Gilbert Smith, and race chief, Joe Craig, after winning the 1952 Junior TT*

*The maestro in race-winning form at Codogno, Italy, 1952*

*Ray Amm and his wife before the start of the 350 cc
North West 200, May 1953. Machine is the
controversial kneeler, nicknamed the 'Flying Fish'*

*Norton private owners' depot, 1953 TT*

which was the first time any road race had ever been
won at over 90 mph.

The following year, in 1936, there were changes
to the frame with the introduction of plunger rear
suspension (nicknamed the 'Garden Gate') in an
attempt to improve the handling. Also the 500's bore
was enlarged by 0.7 mm to give the maximum capacity of 499 cc permitted by FIM regulations, whilst
the 350 was upped to 349 cc (73.4 × 82.5 mm).

Guthrie promptly won the Senior TT and Freddie
Frith, in his first TT, became a star overnight by not
only winning the Junior, but becoming the first man
to do so at over 80 mph.

Craig's team began testing an experimental
engine that year, this was the first double overhead-
camshaft Norton and was adopted on the works
bikes for 1937. And it was with one of the new
double knockers that Frith took the Senior TT at
88.2 mph with the first over 90 mph lap of
90.27 mph. But Nortons were to be shocked when
Jimmy Guthrie suffered a fatal accident whilst leading the German Grand Prix.

In 1938 serious challengers arrived on the scene
from both Germany and Italy in the shape of BMW
and Gilera respectively. Other than AJS, who had

*Ray Amm and works proboscis-faired Norton, Ulster GP 1954. The Rhodesian star scored a double for the Bracebridge Street factory in the event*

developed a supercharged four back in 1935, the British manufacturers, including Norton, hadn't taken advantage of the rules. But both BMW and Gilera *had* made full use of the regulations and the results were machines which, at least in a straight line, were the fastest in the world.

But in road racing, notably the Isle of Man, this wasn't everything as BMW were to find out when they set out to challenge the Bracebridge factory on home ground in the 1938 Senior TT.

Norton had responded to the foreign challenge in their own way—careful development of the existing design. This saw the dohc engine's dimensions changed; the 500 now 82 × 94.3 mm (still 499 cc), whilst the 350 became 75.9 × 77 mm. In addition the bottom half was improved, there were larger cooling fins for the barrel and head and for the first time Norton used telescopic forks (which were undamped).

Unstreamlined and running on a mixture of petrol-benzole with a compression ratio of 11:1, the

*What Norton would have used had the factory not changed its racing policy for the 1955 season—the Guzzi-like horizontal single, known as the F-type*

1938 500 was the quickest Norton yet with a maximum speed of over 120 mph. Output was 52 bhp at 6500 rpm.

Casting the BMW challenge aside Harold Daniell took the Senior TT at 89.1 mph and with a truly sensational performance set a new lap record of 90.99 mph.

But with the threat of war looking greater every day Norton management took the decision that it would pull out of racing—and so 1939 saw Joe Craig leave for BSA (he later went to AMC before returning

Above
*Bob McIntyre with the Joe Potts-tuned 250 Norton. Fitted with a sleeved-down 350 Manx engine, it was good for 100 mph and won many races during 1955 and 1956*

Left
*Yorkshireman Jack Brett leaps Ballaugh Bridge, Senior TT, 1956. He finished third*

to Norton in December 1946). Instead, the Bracebridge Street factory concentrated its efforts on producing WD (War Department) machines, a task it was to carry on for the next seven years. Over 100,000 side-valve models were produced including several hundred sidecar outfits, many with sidecar wheel drive. The works took quite a battering during the conflict, but somehow production was maintained despite the bombing by the *Luftwaffe*.

In 1939 BMW and Gilera shared the spoils of victory, with the German marque scorching to victory in the Senior TT and Dutch TT, and Gilera dominating the German and Ulster GPs. At the latter event Serafina won at 97.5 mph which was the fastest ever road race up to that time. He also set the fastest lap

*Happy faces in the winners' enclosure after the 1955 Junior Manx Grand Prix. Left to right: W. A. Holmes (second) with sponsor Reg Dearden, J. Buchan (fourth), Alan Wilson (Norton race manager), and the winner, G. B. Tanner. All rode Nortons*

of the race at 100.03 mph. But it should also be recalled that Freddie Frith finished second on a 1938 works Norton, averaging a highly impressive 96.83 mph.

For 1940 Norton had planned to offer a pukka racing version of the International which, known as the Manx Grand Prix, would have had a capacity of 499 cc (International was always 490 cc) and telescopic forks as standard. But the war brought this project to a halt even though leaflets were actually printed.

After the end of the conflict Norton decided to 'relaunch' this machine but with the name now shortened to 'Manx'. These were sold fully equipped for racing right down to the last detail. They were coded 30M for the 500 and 40M for the smaller model. The Manx engine used much from the pre-war works unit but was single, rather than double, overhead-camshaft. But although there were a fair number of the new Manx models in circulation it was a Triumph, rather than a Norton, which won the Senior Manx GP in September 1946.

With no TT in 1946, Harold Daniell made his first post-war appearance to win the Senior TT in June 1947. A newcomer to the factory team was Ulsterman Artie Bell who finished second, and was himself the

outright Senior victor in 1948. This was the year which first saw Norton use a twin leading-shoe front brake.

So what you may ask had become of the supercharged challengers? Well, they had been rocked back on their heels with the announcement in 1946, that the fitment of a supercharger could no longer be permitted. This meant that the normally aspirated Nortons were back in the frame. So when classic racing was resumed in 1947 Norton quite literally dug out their 1938 machines and stepped back on the winner's rostrum. The lower speeds which were obtained in the immediate post-war days were due to the need to detune the engines to run on low grade 70 octane pool petrol. This necessitated a drop in compression to some 7:1.

In 1949 the company made the dohc model available for general sale whilst Steve Lancefield was put in charge of the works team. Joe Craig, meanwhile, was tied up for most of the year at Bourne, Lincoln-

*Jack Brett chose to use a pair of Nortons with the 1954 works-type proboscis fairings for the 1957 Junior and Senior TTs*

shire with the BRM racing car team in an attempt to garner enough information to enable Norton to build a four-cylinder design. The year saw AJS and not Norton take the newly introduced 500 cc World Championship title whilst Velocette was triumphant in the 350 title chase.

Norton's only classic win that year was on the Isle of Man when Daniell won the Senior TT. But even then Harold was the first to admit that Les Graham scored a moral victory on the faster AJS Porcupine twin which sheared its magneto three miles from home when leading comfortably. Another twin, a Guzzi ridden by Bob Foster, set the fastest lap at 89.75 mph before retiring.

After the 1949 showing many critics predicted the rapid end of the overhead-cam Norton single. But these very same people were soon to be eating their words, when 20 years after Carroll's engine had made its debut the by now ageing single was reborn. Developed by Rex McCandless in Belfast, with help

from works rider Artie Bell (who was a close friend and business partner), a completely new innovation appeared which was taken on board by the Norton management. This was the 'Featherbed' frame.

Even with basically the same double-knocker single-cylinder engines as before the McCandless designed full duplex frame with its swinging-arm rear suspension set such a high standard of road-holding and handling that it represented a major breakthrough in motorcycle design. This combined with the services of a young rider by the name of Geoff Duke, together with Artie Bell, Harold Daniell and Johnny Lockett, meant that overnight Norton had once again regained the upper hand.

The Featherbed Norton created a sensation when it made its winning debut in Blandford in April 1950. Duke, with his innovative one-piece skin-tight leathers, won the Senior TT at 92.27 mph with Bell and Lockett second and third. And to prove just how competitive Nortons were at that year's TT, Bell, Duke and Daniell also took the first three places in the Junior event.

But then in Belgium and Holland Norton suffered from failures of its Dunlop tyres, and although Duke

*Manx engine on display at the 1958 Earls Court show*

*Checking the run-out on a Manx flywheel assembly, April 1957*

came back to win the 500 cc Ulster and Italian GPs and the 350 cc Italian event he could finish no higher than second in both the World Championship series.

In 1951 Duke made up for these disappointments by scoring a highly impressive championship double with wins in the TT, Belgium, France, Ulster and Italy (350 cc) and the TT, Belgium, Holland and Ulster (500 cc).

The works machines were largely unchanged except for minor details such as the seat, but a change was made to Avon tyres.

The production Manx models now sported the Featherbed frame and several other improvements from the 1950 factory bikes. It is also worth noting that the over-the-counter models were built in a different part of the Bracebridge Street facilities from the works racers and were the responsibility of Edgar Franks.

Meanwhile Joe Craig, nicknamed 'The Wizard of Waft' by a certain well-known pressman, had been busy during the winter of 1951/2, the result being yet a shorter stroke engine for the 500 class, with new bore and stroke measurements of 85.93 × 86 mm. There were other changes too, for both the 500 and 350 in the shape of a Lucas rotating magnet magneto, the first Amal GP carburettor and several smaller improvements to the engine, including cooling fins extended round the vertical drive-shaft tube. The frame now sported a welded-up sub-frame and sintered bronze swinging-arm bushes. Finally a 4.00 × 16 rear tyre on a WM3 alloy rim was tried on the 500 at early season meetings.

Strangely, these changes seemed to benefit the smaller model most, with Duke winning the first four Grands Prix before a serious accident at a non-championship event at Schotten, Germany ruined his season. Even so, those four wins were good enough to retain the 350 cc crown. But there was no such luck in the larger class, as the season had got off badly for the defending champion, with his highest place being second in both the Dutch and Belgian rounds, before his accident.

By the end of the 1952 season it was evident that in the Gilera 500 four the Italians had the fastest bike. But in Duke, Norton had the fastest rider.

That winter Duke publicly criticized Norton racing policy which upset the company's managing director Gilbert Smith. This resulted in Smith promoting the Rhodesian, Ray Amm, to team leader, backed up by the Australian Ken Kavanagh and Englishman Syd Lawton. It should also be noted that the winner of the 1952 Senior TT on a Norton, Reg Armstrong, had already agreed to join Gilera for 1953.

*Phil Read receiving the Junior TT trophy after winning the 1961 event on his Norton single*

*Read amazed the racegoers by splitting the works Gilera fours with his Lancefield Norton at Silverstone in April 1963*

Above left and right
*'King of Brands', Derek Minter, and 'Mooneyes' John Cooper—two of the leading British short-circuit stars of the 1960s. Both campaigned Norton singles*

This effectively left Duke without a factory ride. First he attempted to 'rejoin' Norton, a move which was stupidly turned down by the management, then right on the eve of the new season finally signed for Gilera as team leader.

From that time onwards the fate of the racing Norton at factory level was sealed. And although they still won on occasion—for example a TT double by Amm in 1953 and a final Senior TT victory for the Rhodesian in 1954, the writing was clearly on the wall. The result was that Norton, now owned by AMC, declared that support was too costly and their future effort would be made with prototype production versions of the Manx. This move sidelined the proposed projects which had included a new single with the cylinder horizontal in Guzzi fashion, and further into the future a dohc four-cylinder.

But before leaving the works models to look at the new 1955 team on production prototypes it is worth recalling some of the factory's other achievements prior to their changing emphasis. Top of the list must come the five World Sidecar Championships. Four of these went to Eric Oliver (1949, 1950, 1951 and 1953), the other going to Cyril Smith (1952). Then there were the successful record-breaking sprees at Montlhéry in 1949 and 1953, and also the many pre-war efforts. Finally, mention must be made of the fully streamlined 'Flying Fish' kneeler of 1953 which was conceived by the designer of the Featherbed frame, Rex McCandless. Controversy rages to this very day on just how good or bad the

*Ray Petty's back-to-front 350 Manx, 1963. It was later ridden with a considerable degree of success by Derek Minter*

Overleaf
*Senior TT 1967. Chris Conn and John Cooper at Keppel Gate*

*John Tickle took over the Manx business from Colin Seeley in 1969. He is pictured here with one of his 500 cc Tickle T5 Manx machines in 1971. Very few were actually produced*

kneeler really was. In an article published in the December 1984 issue of *Classic Bike* its creator stated that: 'Because the kneeler was not Craig's idea, he was always against it', and cited this as the reason the project didn't progress further than it did. Whereas factory rider Ken Kavanagh (who did the early testing at Montlhéry) says that Ray Amm, after two or three laps in TT practice didn't want to race the streamliner, and with Lawton out through injury Craig could not afford to have one of his riders on an experimental bike in the TT.

But whatever the case the speed potential of the streamliner kneeler was clearly shown when Amm *averaged* 134 mph to set a new world hour record later that year at Montlhéry. Kavanagh also revealed to me that it was some 20 mph faster than the conventional Featherbed framed model. However, once again, speed has to be matched with handling . . .

The 1955 team comprised Surtees, Hartle and Brett and although they put up some good performances at home, in the classics the going was much

more difficult and the best result was Hartle's pair of second places in the Ulster GP. However, the non-championship Swedish GP saw the Norton team riders take the first three places in the 350 cc race (Hartle, Surtees and Brett). But this was to be their swansong as Surtees quit to join MV and in December the long-serving Joe Craig retired.

There then followed a period when Doug Hele (later such an influential figure at Triumph) took over where Craig had left off, continuing the almost yearly list of improvements. These included AMC gearboxes, sodium-cooled valves, modified cams, redesigned con-rod and big-end assemblies, revised vertical drive to cam gear and many more alterations—even experiments with desmodromic heads.

Then there were the efforts of the private tuners, men like Lancefield, Beart and Petty, who continued to extract more power even into the 1960s.

The year 1961 had seen a final Junior/Senior TT victory, when Phil Read and Mike Hailwood respectively benefited from the retirement of the factory MVs of Gary Hocking in both races. Production of the Manx came to an end around this time, although a few machines were built from existing stocks in 1962. But private owners would not forsake what they saw as the most ideal machine for the job, and both on the British short circuits, and on the Isle of Man the Manx continued to prove its capabilities year after year.

The list of achievements gained by the privately-owned Manx racers is almost endless, but suffice to say it created many world renowned riders, men such as Derek Minter, John Cooper, Dan Shorey and Chris Conn, to name but a few.

However, a major problem was to arise, that of spare parts. Perhaps the lowest ebb was reached when Colin Seeley bought the manufacturing rights from AMC but chose to concentrate his production on the Matchless G50 and AJS 7R. The subsequent appearance of new Seeley machines with these power units made it look as if the Manx Norton was finally finished. But late in 1969, John Tickle acquired the Manx business and things began to roll again. The same year Londoner Godfrey Nash became the last rider to win a classic Grand Prix on a British bike when he took the chequered flag in the 500 cc Yugoslav GP on his Manx.

But the final development was to be Leighton Buzzard dealer/tuner Sid Mularney's four-valve model. Built in 1970 it is perhaps the only Manx capable of beating the hoard of AMC-based racers at classic racing events today.

# 4
# Matchless G45 and G50

The racing history of Matchless is unusual for it is split into two distinct periods—pre-World War 1 and post-World War 2—with a period of over 30 years of almost complete inactivity between them.

It was in the very earliest days of the sport that the name Matchless first came to the fore through the exploits of the Collier brothers Charlie and Harry, who were members of the family that founded the company. They formed an almost unbeatable combination in the road and track races of their time, riding together or singly in the three International Cup Races up to 1907 and between them winning three TTs. They were placed four times between 1907 and 1914—exclusively on Matchless machinery. In fact, the very first TT race in 1907 was won by Charlie Collier.

After World War 1, apart from the brief and unsuccessful appearance in 1923 of a 350 cc ohc Matchless, the marque withdrew its support for racing until 1951. Then in the Manx Grand Prix that September Robin Sherry rode the prototype of what was to emerge as the G45 racing twin. Sherry was to finish the Senior event in fourth spot at an average speed of 83.7 mph, although towards the end of the

*Robin Sherry taking the prototype Matchless G45 twin to victory in the Senior Manx Grand Prix, September 1951*

*A G45 on show at Earls Court*

race he slowed when one of the rocker pillars broke, which caused a considerable amount of unwanted vibration. In the 1952 TT the same bike was ridden again by the Australian rider, Ernie Ring, who was forced to retire after falling on lap 5.

A year after its competition debut the new racing Matchless came up trumps in the Senior Manx GP ridden by Derek Farrant (the same machine used by Ring in the TT). The Matchless twin not only won the race but also set new race and lap records at 88.65 and 89.64 mph respectively.

Following this success AMC finally decided to make the new machine available to the general public in the same way as it had already done with the AJS 7R (see Chapter 1) and to this end a prototype was displayed at Earls Court that November.

The G45 (the 45 part of the designation being in respect of its original planned output of 45 bhp) was the work of H.J. (Ike) Hatch and was placed in 'production' during early 1953.

Apart from the cylinder heads and barrels, the engine closely resembled the Matchless (and AJS) roadster twins which had been announced back in late 1948, the Matchless G9 and AJS Model 20. And, in fact, the G45 shared the same 498 cc, 66 × 72.8 mm long-stroke bore and stroke measurements.

To cope with the increased power, the crankshaft was an alloy steel forging with shrunk-on flywheel rims. The plain middle main bearing was slightly narrower than hitherto but the other main bearings, of the roller pattern, and the light-alloy con-rods were standard. The high compression, die-cast pistons had solid skirts and carried two compression rings and a slotted scraper ring. The wire-winding on the G9/Model 20 pistons was not featured for racing, since mechanical noise was unimportant.

Timing gear and oil pump were based on standard components, but the camshafts were not. In conjunction with roller-type followers and special overhead rockers, they provided more overlap and quicker valve opening and closing than the G9/Model 20 layout. Pushrods were light alloy tubes of $\frac{3}{8}$ in. outside diameter, each having a hardened-steel ball at the lower end and a hardened-steel cup at the top. Bronze-bushed rockers provided diagonal, straight-line operation between pushrod and valve stem. Adjustment of valve clearances was effected by eccentrically mounted rocker spindles, as on the standard engine.

Triple helical valve springs were employed; each had a two-rate winding to minimize surge. Inlet valve diameter was $1\frac{17}{32}$ in., and that of the exhaust valve $1\frac{13}{32}$ in.—both larger than the roadster power unit. The rockers bore directly on the valve stems, which were Stellite tipped. The valve guides were phosphor bronze. Barrels and heads were separate for each cylinder and were of light alloy, with deep finning. The barrels had shrunk-in liners which extended well down into the crankcase. Austenitic iron inlet and bronze exhaust valve seats were also shrunk into position. Electron was used for the rocker covers; the finning on the exhaust covers was largely responsible for the different appearance of the unit compared to the G9. The covers were retained by studs and nuts, whereas the standard engine had bolts which screwed into the head.

Transmission was through a Burman racing gear-box and the engine-shaft shock absorber was replaced by rubber blocks in the clutch centre. Two Amal GP carburettors (fed by a single, remotely mounted float chamber) and a Lucas racing magneto were also specified.

Gearbox of the Smiths magnetic rev-counter was driven from the near-side end of the exhaust cam-shaft, and not from the magneto pinion as on the prototypes. Both the fuel and oil tanks were of light alloy, and had capacities of six gallons and one gallon respectively.

Frame, suspension and brakes were virtually identical to the 1953 AJS 7R, as were the cycle parts generally, including such features as the fuel tank mounting and system of chain lubrication. An exception was the tyre sizes which were 3.00 at the front and 3.50 at the rear. To ensure that the exhaust pipes cleared the frame the port angle was wider than on the standard engine.

Very little modification was made to the machine throughout its life, but a mini redesign of the engine

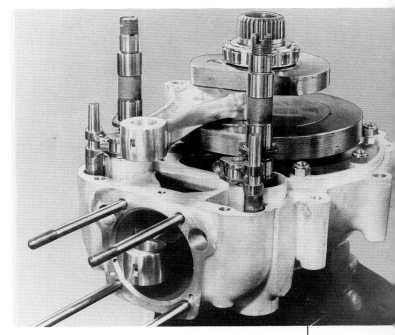

**Top right**
*G45 crankcases and cylinder barrels*

**Centre right**
*Crankcases split to show the crankshaft*

**Right**
*Camshaft details*

for the 1956 model saw the introduction of new head castings to incorporate strengthened rocker posts and stronger valve springs. Oil leakage from the cylinder base was cured by an improved O-ring whilst the big-end studs were increased in diameter.

In fact, the G45 engine generally proved reliable, except for a series of broken pushrods, especially on the exhaust side.

But the Achilles' heel of the design was its narrow power band, which meant that only the most gifted riders could really get the best from it. When this happened it was liable to put in an excellent performance. Three performances in particular are noteworthy. One was at the Dutch TT in 1955 when the Australian Bob Brown finished fifth after a long and thrilling tussle with Umberto Masetti (MV four)—remember that Brown was on a privately-entered unfaired production pushrod twin, whilst the Italian was on a works fully faired, four-cylinder! Another was a pair of sixth places in the Senior TT of 1955 and 1956 by Manxman Derek Ennett, which included a fastest lap of over 96 mph. Finally, New Zealander Peter Murphy won many races aboard the Plumstead twin including the Senior class of the New Zealand Grand Prix in 1957 and 1958.

But after Hatch's death in 1954 the factory largely lost interest in the G45, and it was finally replaced by the single-cylinder G50. Two of these machines first appeared during the 1958 season, ridden by Peter Ferbache and Jack Ahearn and were developed from the 350 AJS 7R, to which it owed obvious allegiance. The stroke, indeed, remained the same at 78 mm but the bore was enlarged to 90 mm, giving a capacity of 496 cc. The only external difference was that outside plumbing was used for the pressure feed-pipe to the cam gear and the fore and aft drains from the rocker boxes. Carburettor was a $1\frac{1}{2}$ in. Amal GP. Valve sizes on these prototypes were as on the 7R, as was the part-sphere of the combustion space. The piston crown hump was thus considerably smaller than the bore, so that squish was provided as the piston approached tdc. During 1958 the engine was purely experimental with AMC chief development engineer Jack Williams hard at work to perfect it, so it would be ready to go on sale for the 1959 season. Once again the original idea had come from sales director Jock West.

When it entered production the G50 had purpose-built castings, rather than the reworked 7R components. This meant that instead of 49 bhp at

*Frank Perris (65) leads on his G45 at Ibsley, August 1955*

*The G45 sidecar outfit of Fritz Staschel at the 1954 German GP. Note that the sidecar brake was operated hydraulically from the rear brake control*

7000 rpm (claimed) of the prototypes the 1959 version gave 51 bhp at 7200 rpm.

For 1960 engine alterations included closer adjustment to the vernier ignition timing, a stronger magneto strap, more rigid float chamber mounting brackets and larger $1\frac{7}{8}$ in. diameter inlet valve, instead of a $1\frac{3}{4}$ in. component.

The following year the changes were essentially limited to very minor alterations such as an alteration to the shape of the timing chest to enable an exhaust pipe with a better curve to be fitted and tucked in closer. There were also alterations to the front forks, with the replacement of the two springs formerly used in each leg by a single multi-rate spring. Damping characteristics were altered to match. The fork oil seals were now double-lipped, the outer lips wiping and cleaning the fork stanchions to minimize the ingress of dirt and grit. Also, the metal fork covers were replaced by rubber gaiters for weight-saving and greater cleanliness. Fork travel was increased. Other detail changes affected the rear suspension units, front brake and oil filler cap. By now the price had increased to

£455 19s 3d (the 7R cost £443 5s 11d).

In total AMC built some 180 G50s before production ended in 1962, plus 50 examples of the G50 CSR. The latter machine was a street-legal version for sale in America. The reason for this was not really to offer the ultimate sports roadster, but to comply with AMA (American Motorcycle Association) rules regarding the Daytona 200. AMA rules stated that at least 25 roadster-based machines had to be sold before a model could be approved for racing.

Almost the only concession to 'road' use was the fitment of a smaller Amal GP2 carburettor of $1\frac{3}{8}$ in. diameter, compared to the $1\frac{1}{2}$ in. choke size of the pukka racer. With an AMC silencer installed, Matchless claimed an output of 46.5 bhp at 7000 rpm. And with the silencer and 'high-and-wide' Stateside bars said it would achieve 110 mph.

When the AMA competition committee approved the G50 CSR for racing in early November 1961 it was with both the heavy roadster-based lugged and brazed CSR frame *and* the all-welded G50 road-racing assembly.

The machine (in full road-racing trim!) created a massive stir at its Stateside debut, when Dick Mann finished second in the 1962 Daytona Classic, only feet behind Don Bunett on a works Triumph twin. By the end of that season Mann only missed winning

Above
*1961 Matchless G50 single*

Right
*G50 engine with magneto and Amal GP carburettor*

the coveted AMA Number One Plate after an accident on the Springfield mile dirt-track.

But 1963 saw the combination of Mann and the G50 become champions, before AMA officials took action to ban the bike—so the native Harley 750 side-valve twins could stand a chance of winning again . . .

In Europe the G50 never really achieved the success of the Manx Norton in the early 1960s. Although after it was taken out of production in 1962 things improved, thanks in no small part to the efforts of a certain Tom Kirby.

Kirby, who ran a motorcycle dealership in Horn-church, Essex, began his involvement with the sport by sponsoring the up-and-coming Alf Hagon in grass-track events. But looking for fresh pastures in 1961, he bought a new 7R and G50 on which to sponsor one of his mechanics, Ernie Wooder. In 1962 AMC decided to lend Kirby a few development

Above
*Derek Woodman with the G50 on which he gained second place in the 1964 Southern 100. The machine is completely standard except for the MZ front brake*

Below
*A 500 cc dice, Austrian Grand Prix, 1965. Jack Findlay with the legendary McIntyre Matchless leads Norton riders Chris Conn and Jack Ahearn*

*John Blanchard taking his Seeley Matchless to an excellent second place in the 500 cc race at the 1967 North West 200*

Previous page
*Derek Minter thunders past the pits on his 500 Seeley Matchless, Snetterton, 20 March 1966*

bikes. One result which springs to mind is Robin Dawson's Junior Manx Grand Prix victory that year. Now staking everything in road-racing, Kirby engaged no fewer than five riders for 1963, had eight race machines on his books and two factory bikes on loan. Their riders were Alan Shepherd, Paddy Driver, Lewis Young, Ron Chandler and Roger Hunter. Shepherd finished runner-up in the 500 cc World Championship and gave Kirby his biggest moment till then by beating both factory Gilera fours in the Race of the Year at Mallory Park that September.

Perhaps the greatest year for the Kirby équipe was 1964, when they were knee deep in riders—

*Colin Seeley was not the only one to offer an alternative chassis for the 7R and G50 engine. There was also the Rickman Metisse, shown here in February 1966*

seven in all, with 14 machines, plus spares. For Grand Prix events the team was Phil Read, Paddy Driver and Jack Findley. Whilst for the home circuits Lewis Young, Joe Dunphy, Ron Chandler and Roger Hunter did the business. In less than three seasons Tom Kirby had achieved his aim of fielding the biggest, most successful, private racing team in Britain, probably in the world.

Later, other stars such as Bill Ivy and even Mike Hailwood rode the Kirby AMC machinery to victory. Besides the Kirby effort several other sponsors kept the Matchless G50 alive though none more so than Tom Arter. His chief rider Peter Williams won

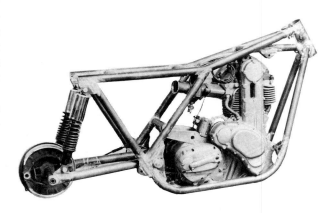

undying fame for his efforts over several years and between 1967 and 1973 Williams finished second in the Senior TT on no less than four occasions.

The other significant event connected with the G50 in Britain during this period involved Colin Seeley who was a sidecar racer of considerable note and had close links with AMC through his use of G50 and race-tuned G12 CSR engines. Seeley made the bold move in 1965 to start manufacturing racing motorcycles. It was a reasonably small start as he came to an agreement with AMC, who had announced that after 1965 they did not wish to be involved with the racing side of the business.

So for 1966 Seeley created his own 7R and G50 powered racers, the first ones being raced by Derek Minter (although a couple of frame kits had already been supplied to other riders). But although the machines were quickly accepted two problems soon surfaced, the first was a financial loss that year for the Seeley organization, and secondly, hard on the heels of this news was that AMC had decided to quit production of the engines. Undeterred by these matters Colin Seeley decided to go the whole hog

and buy out the AMC racing department! As well as the Matchless and AJS stock he also acquired the Manx Norton side of the business but later sold this to John Tickle (see Chapter 3).

There is no doubt that this was the right move as the financial side of things improved and in any case if Seeley had not purchased the AMC racing business and started producing his own engines it is highly doubtful that his own operation could have survived.

From 1967 onwards things really boomed with not only a relatively large number of machines, engines and frame kits being sold, but Dave Croxford won the British championship in 1968 and 1969 on Seeley G50 machines.

The G50 was the mainstay of the business as the 7R was soon dropped and Seeley cashed in on the 350 Yamaha by introducing the Yamsel frame that John Cooper helped to develop.

*Alan Barnett exits the Governor's Bridge dip with his 500 Kirby Metisse to take second place in the 1969 Senior TT*

*Peter Williams in race-winning form on the Tom Arter G50 at Mallory Park, 26 March 1967*

*With the emergence of classic racing in the 1980s, the G50 has been the bike to beat. Former World Champion Hugh Anderson (centre) is one rider to have displayed race-winning form. The New Zealander is shown here at Oulton Park in October 1985*

Probably the best Seeley G50 results on the Isle of Man came in 1969 when Tom Dickie, Derek Woodman and Ron Chandler finished third, fourth and sixth in the Senior TT.

On the short circuits besides Croxford's championship victories, John Cooper and Alan Barnett were second in 1967 and 1970 respectively.

The Irish North West 200 was a happy hunting ground for the Seeley G50. Cooper won in 1968 and John Blanchard in 1969.

By 1970 Seeley employed some 16 full-time staff, many of whom were ex-AMC employees. The same year ex-Honda and Bultaco star Tommy Robb brought his privately-owned Seeley G50 home fourth in the 500 cc World Championships. But from then on things were never quite the same as slowly but surely the two-strokes, such as the overbored Yamaha twins, Kawasaki three and finally the Suzuki RG500, sealed the British single's fate as the 1970s progressed. And with it went the possibility of the G50 as a viable racing engine.

But a decade later the design was reborn, this time as a prime mover in the classic racing scene. Today the G50 is acknowledged as the top engine in the 500 cc category and several companies are involved in either offering spares or even complete replica machines.

# 5
# Norton—the JPS saga

The Norton Commando made its debut at the 1967 Earls Court Show and with it came a new name, Norton-Villiers, backed by Manganese Bronze, with former car racer Dennis Poore as its Chairman. But the subject of this chapter, the John Player Norton racing story, really began after Peter Williams (son of the famous AMC development engineer Jack) joined Norton-Villiers in 1969 with an enviable track record and also the reputation of being a first-class engineer. The following year Williams came within a hair's breadth of winning the prestigious Production TT on the Isle of Man but with Malcolm Uphill's Triumph in his sights his Norton Commando ran low on fuel and Williams was forced to accept second spot.

*Peter Williams aboard the Commando, which he shared with Charlie Sanby to win the 1970 Thruxton 500-mile race*

The TT performance really summed up the Norton effort in 1970 with the BSA and Triumph triples taking much of the glory, even though Williams and the Commando notched up numerous wins and places in production events throughout Britain.

The Commando stemmed from the 497 cc Dominator, designed by Bert Hopwood, whilst Norton were still in their original Bracebridge Street, Birmingham, home during the early 1950s. The next change was to 596 cc as the Model 99 and then the 646 cc Dominator 650SS which was introduced in the early 1960s.

Then in the mid 1960s the capacity was boosted once again, this time to 745 cc (73 × 89 mm) to become the Atlas. Although the Commando also used this engine size for its first five years of production (and also for racing purposes), the new model departed in several ways from the layout of its predecessors.

*Debut day for the new 750 Norton F1 racer, 1971*

The most noticeable changes were that the engine was canted forward several degrees from the vertical and a totally new frame was adopted. A feature of this was its rubber mountings, more commonly known as Isolastic mounts.

This is essentially the machine which Williams had raced in 1970. However, he persuaded the company to allow the construction of a full racing version, rather than the previous production machine. The result first appeared at a Crystal Palace meeting in 1971. The bike was clearly intended to compete in the new Formula 750 class. Norton's management were sufficiently satisfied not only to allow its further development, but to actively seek outside sponsorship. And it was Chairman Dennis Poore who himself made contact with the giant Imperial Tobacco company. This was a fortuitous move as it coincided with Imperial's desire to find a sponsorship outlet in a field previously barren to cigarette and tobacco advertising.

The sponsorship deal was soon cemented and not only was the team named John Player Norton with Williams as its chief rider and development engineer, but Poore introduced the former Suzuki and AMC star Frank Perris to the proceedings as team manager. Wishing to make the maximum impact for the 1972 season the team also signed up Phil Read and Tony Rutter as additional riders. And it was Williams and Read who were to contest the John Player Norton's first meeting, the Daytona 200.

The machines were powered by tuned Commando Combat engines, producing 69 bhp at 7500 rpm. These were equipped with twin Amal GP carbs, and fitted in Commando-based frames, designed by Williams, which retained the large diameter top tube and Isolastic mounts of the original.

Equipped with Norvil forks and double Lockheed discs at the front, the two Daytona machines were wrapped in a comprehensive fairing, which had been developed at MIRA's (Motor Industry Research Association) wind-tunnel near Nuneaton, Warwickshire, and, resplendent in a distinctive royal blue and white finish, the bikes certainly looked impressive.

In order to carry 24 litres of fuel, without jacking the centre of gravity up too high, pannier tanks were fitted. These partially enveloped the engine and were shaped so as to allow the riders to tuck away as much as possible.

Testing had revealed certain shortcomings, the most serious was an over-heavy front end, which

**Above**
*One of the two John Player Nortons entered for Daytona, March 1972*

**Below**
*Team rider Mick Grant and JPS bikes at Snetterton, Race of Aces, 1972*

would manifest itself if the power was turned on too sharply coming out of a corner, when the rear wheel had a nasty habit of getting out of line.

At Daytona, both Williams and Read exceeded 150 mph in practice, with Read fastest at 155.17 mph but still slower than the BSA and Triumph triples. Even so, in the race good handling and torque came more into their own with Read leading at one stage, before finally having to settle for fourth spot and $2200. He was on the first four-stroke behind a trio of Yamaha TZ350 'strokers. Meanwhile Williams had been well up until he was forced out with gearbox problems.

The following month Read again finished fourth, this time the location was Imola, Italy, and the first of the now famous 200-mile races. The same month Rutter had quit the team, to be replaced by the up-and-coming star, Yorkshireman Mick Grant.

Then came perhaps the main event of the year for the JPS team, the Isle of Man TT series. In the Production event Williams lost some 35 seconds frantically trying to kickstart his machine into life. Perhaps it was that he was trying harder than usual but the machine lost fourth gear and the Norton man

*JPS team for 1973: Frank Perris (team manager) and riders Croxford, Cooper and Williams*

had to be content with second place behind the winning Trident.

But at the time the team didn't seem to mind as they still had the F750 race and with it the prospect of three top runners, Williams, Read and John Cooper, to show the world that Norton was back in a big way.

Unfortunately for everyone concerned with the

*Mick Woollett, Peter Bryan, Dave Croxford, Mick Grant and Dennis Poore. Croxford and Grant had just won the Thruxton 500-miler, 1 October 1972*

*A 1973 racer, showing bodywork to advantage*

Norton effort the race was a disaster, as all three bikes were sidelined after two laps. This was to be a feature for much of the season, with gearboxes causing the biggest headache. Both the production and F750 bikes were equipped with Quaife five-speeders. The fault lay with the primary drive layout, with the triplex chain pulling hard on the mainshaft bending it out of line so that teeth were broken off the gears on both the mainshaft and the layshaft, particularly in respect of first and second.

Towards the end of the year, however, things began to brighten considerably. Grant gave the team its first victory at Scarborough in September, whilst a month later Percy Tait and Dave Croxford won the Thruxton 500-miler on a production Commando. Later that month at Brands Hatch, Read scored a much publicized victory, with Williams taking third place. At the same time Croxford had his first F750 race on a John Player Norton. This resulted in the decision to contract Croxford, who joined Williams in the team for the 1973 season.

Non-stop development work took place in the winter of 1972–3 as the JPS team strove to improve the machines. The most important change was in

*Inside the Norton workshop at Andover, 13 January 1973. Left to right: Peter Williams, Rodney Clist and Frank Perris. The bike is a 1973 model JPS racer*

*The 1974 JPS chassis and engine details*

the shape of the new monocoque chassis which, although it stemmed from an idea put forward by Peter Williams, was actually the work of ace welder Rodney Clist. Basically, this was a double-skinned creation in mild steel incorporating both the fuel and oil tanks, together with other items such as fairing brackets. When one considers that its total weight was only 37 lb and that an even lighter, thinner gauge stainless-steel version was also built, this was a significant achievement.

From a visual angle the latest bikes looked even better, with a brand new fairing, tank and seat, and finished in a distinctive white, set off with blue and red striping. Underneath this new exterior a considerable amount of effort had been expended in improving the engine, gearbox and suspension. For a start there were new leading-axle forks, with the team's own sliders fitted with AJS Stormer motocross stanchions and yokes which improved high-speed handling. The engine was mounted further back in the frame resulting in a more balanced bike with a low centre of gravity which instilled rider confidence.

But having a machine with superb handling was only half the equation and so the long-stroke push-

rod engine was breathed upon. This included altered valve angles and larger valves, a higher lift camshaft, which alone provided an extra 2 bhp and stronger valve springs. The alloy pushrods were replaced by steel components, which might appear to have been

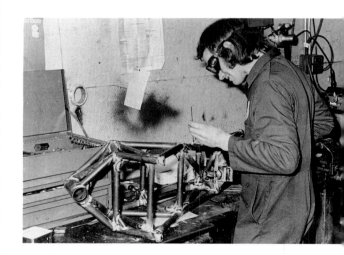

Above
*Ace welder Clist in action with 1974-type frame*

Right
*Williams was in a class of his own when winning the 1973 Formula 1 TT*

*Williams and Croxford, plus Suzuki-mounted Barry Sheene, battle for honours at Brands Hatch*

a backwards step—but it was found that the alloy ones were prone to compress and expand at high rpm.

Another area which received attention was the primary drive, and in an attempt to solve the problems in this area a new primary chaincase with a third bearing was installed. In addition, dished sprockets were provided to direct the load on to this bearing, rather than as previously the shaft, while the shock absorber was transferred from the gearbox end of the crankshaft and an external dry clutch was fitted.

The combination of changes added up to the 1973 engine which offered a healthy 78 bhp at 7400 rpm. This at last provided the team with a competitive machine which had an excellent combination of speed and handling.

Even though the JPS team got off to a poor start at Daytona, after that the winter's work paid off dividends with a string of victories and places that summer. The first signs of just how competitive the new bike was came in the Easter match race series, where Peter Williams was the highest points scorer with four wins.

But it was at the TT, where Williams romped away to victory in the Formula 750 TT at an average speed of 105.47 mph for the five-lap race, that even

the critics began singing praises. This could have been the second TT success that year for Williams if his production JPS Commando hadn't broken down whilst in the lead.

Norton also entered several of the year's long-distance endurance events including the Barcelona 24 hours, Bol d'Or and the Thruxton 500-miler. In the last event Nortons came first and second.

To cap a truly superb year, Dave Croxford became British road-race champion—a fitting tribute to both man and machine. Both had had their ups and downs over the years but when things were going right both proved they could deliver the goods.

But it was back to reality with a bang in 1974 when the two-stroke Formula 750s really came into their own. All at once the four-strokes were, in a word, outclassed. This didn't just apply to Norton, but to the likes of the Ducati V-twin and Triumph/BSA triples too.

But the John Player team did at least try to compete and during the closed season built an almost entirely new bike. Gone was the monocoque chassis and long-stroke engine and in its place came a new nickel-plated space-frame in 20 gauge Reynolds 531 tubing, with an equally new shorter stroke version of the venerable pushrod twin with bore and stroke measurements of 77 × 80 mm, giving 80 bhp.

However, 1974 was to prove a bitter disappointment to everyone concerned with the JPS team, now with additional backing from the Gulf Oil Company.

Although claimed to be some 50 lb lighter than the 1973 model, the new bike with its shorter stroke engine didn't live up to expectations where it mattered—out on the circuits—and to prove this lap times were actually *slower*. Although Williams did win the Hutchinson 100, other performances were far less satisfactory. For example, in the TT both JPSs were to retire on the first lap! If this was not bad enough on a fateful day in August, Williams suffered a serious accident, which finished his racing career, after the fibreglass mountings for the tank broke causing him to lose control at Oulton Park.

Even though Croxford struggled away against the two-stroke menace it was now evident that the day of the Commando-based racer was over. At the end of the season the John Player sponsorship was withdrawn. The one light at the end of the tunnel was the promise of a brand new engine, made for Norton by the Cosworth concern.

Cosworth's brief was to design and build 25 750 cc parallel twin engines which could be used for F750 racing and in the future could, with little modification, be offered in a sports roadster. The power unit was based on the Northampton company's DFV V8 Formula 1 car engine, which at the time was the best engine in Grand Prix racing, four-wheel style. The 3-litre V8 was developing 470 bhp and so both Norton and Cosworth believed that a twin—a quarter of that—would produce some 118 bhp. Even allowing for mechanical losses in the conver-

*The ill-fated Cosworth dohc engine*

sion 100 bhp should have been possible. So much for the theory, the engine had bore and stroke measurements of $85.73 \times 64.77$ mm when completed, giving a capacity of 746.88 cc.

The dohc heads used four valves per cylinder and with an included valve angle of only 32 degrees the combustion chamber was extremely compact. The forged pistons had a high compression ratio of $12:1$, but the top was virtually flat with shallow valve cutaways and a squish band machined into it. A central spark plug fed by Lucas Rita electronic ignition, combined with the compact combustion chamber meant that flame travel was notably short.

Watercooling was necessary to ensure a constant operating temperature for this advanced unit. To smooth the inherent vibrations of a twin-cylinder layout a pair of contra-rotating balancer shafts were fitted and behind the rear shaft there was provision for an electric start for the proposed roadster version.

Primary drive was courtesy of a Morse Hy-Vo inverted tooth chain which, although heavier than the standard roller type, was also much more robust. The diaphragm clutch featured sintered metal plates.

The gearbox was a five-speeder but was unusual for a British motorcycle with its indirect drive. The crankcase assembly incorporated a huge lug for the swinging-arm pivot behind the gearbox.

Extensive bench testing confirmed the 100 bhp potential with fuel injection but conventional carburettors did not suit the Cosworth twin and power output with these was considerably lower.

The new Norton Cosworth made its race debut on a Saturday afternoon at Brands Hatch in October 1975 but a first corner mêlée saw rider Croxford and the new bike eliminated together with many others. Croxford was injured in the accident so Alex George was quickly drafted into the squad as a replacement but the following day the Scot was destined to retire in a lowly 20th spot. Even so, he voiced his opinion that 'with a winter of development I feel it could be a winner'.

This was not to be, however, as disappointing results in the early 1976 meetings saw the whole project abandoned, together with the Norton team.

And so a period of five years, in which the Norton name had again hit the headlines, came to an end—sometimes with victory, sometimes in defeat, but always grabbing the observer's attention.

Over a decade later a new works Norton team was to emerge with the controversial Wankel rotary engine, and once again close involvement with the John Player name . . . but that's another story.

# 6
# Porcupine and
# 3-Valve

## Porcupine

Strangely, the AJS Porcupine was originally the brainchild of the man largely responsible for the development of the works single-cylinder Nortons, Joe Craig.

Just prior to World War 2, Craig left the famous Bracebridge Street concern, first going to BSA and then on to AMC (Associated Motorcycles) in Plumstead, south-east London. And so Craig came to spend the war years at AMC. The reason the famous Norton race supremo of the 1930s had left his beloved tuning shrine at Bracebridge Street in January 1939 was his frustration at Norton's racing policy for that year—in which they had decided to

*The original E90 Porcupine twin made its debut in the spring of 1947, its name being coined from the spiky finning on the cylinder head*

concentrate on motorcycles for the coming conflict, rather than those on which to go racing. So as a protest Craig upped and left. When he finally arrived at AMC they had already developed the extremely fast, but largely unreliable, watercooled V4 on which Walter Rusk had become the first man to lap the Ulster GP at over 100 mph in August 1939, before being forced to retire with a broken girder fork leg.

Craig convinced the Collier brothers (owners of AMC at that time) to abandon the V4 in favour of a new twin, code-named the E90. Because Craig was not a designer in the true sense but a development engineer it meant that the detail drawings and design work were in fact carried out by Phil Irving and Vic Webb.

In many ways its design was far in advance of anything else conceived in Britain during the 1940s, but its full potential was never to be realized because it was built for supercharging and when the FIM banned blowers in 1947 the E90, soon to be nicknamed the 'Porcupine', was at a major disadvantage from the outset of its career the same year.

The first the world heard of the new racer was in May 1947, when AMC invited pressmen down to their Plumstead factory for the official launch.

*1949 500 cc World Champion Les Graham in vivid action on his Porcupine at that year's Belgian GP*

Overleaf
*AJS works team in the 1951 500 cc Ulster GP: Armstrong (10), Doran (9) and Coleman (52)*

Below
*The first 500 cc World Championship title went to Englishman Les Graham, a real gentleman of the sport*

*In 1952 the revised E95 Porcupine arrived. This had several differences, most notably a completely revised engine canted at 45 degrees*

Details appeared in the 29 May issue of both *The Motor Cycle* and *Motor Cycling*.

The Porcupine's engine was of unit construction—itself a rarity in Britain at that time—and the near square 68 mm bore and 68.5 mm stroke gave a capacity of 499 cc. The twin overhead camshafts were driven by a train of gears which also actuated the oil pump and magneto.

The side-by-side cylinders lay 15 degrees above the horizontal. The widely spaced camboxes, which also contained the overlapping hairpin valve springs, formed a large catchment for cooling air (needed for the original use of a supercharger). But this gave a problem of getting enough air to cool the barrels which were somewhat hidden by the heads and camboxes. The head finning with its 'spikes' was what had led to the name Porcupine.

All engine castings other than the heads and barrels were of magnesium alloy and unlike contemporary parallel twins, the crankshaft machined from a

single steel forging, had three bearings, the centre one being a plain journal to which oil was fed and from which the linered split plain big-ends in the light-alloy con-rods were lubricated.

Primary drive was by straight-cut gears, and the engine ran backwards, with the clutch, which ran at 80 per cent of engine speed, being located outside the drive casing and so liberally drilled for aircooling that *Motor Cycling* said it 'closely resembles a crumpet'! The four-speed close ratio gearbox was of conventional design, except that it had a 'crossover' drive with the rear chain on the off-side, whilst the clutch withdrawal mechanism was housed outside the final-drive sprocket.

The lubrication was efficient . . . and powerful. This special system worked as follows: one pump supplied oil to the mains and big-ends whilst another, housed in the same body and located above the crankcase, supplied jets which were applied directly on to each cam face. Oil from the crankcase was returned by a pump in the sump, this disposition of pumps being intended to avoid the possibility of heat interchange between outgoing and ingoing oil, which is bound to occur where pressure and scavenge pumps are formed in the same body in the conventional manner.

In its original form (without a supercharger!) the Porcupine engine gave 40 bhp at 7600 rpm.

A full duplex cradle frame, with swinging-arm rear suspension, had the AMC teledraulic front forks, which were based around those pioneered on the War Department 350 Matchless single used extensively during the war. The rear units were of the oil and air type.

The debut for the newcomer came in the TT of all places, where Les Graham and the veteran Jock West, now AMC sales manager, were entered in the Senior.

During practice they soon discovered the machine's deficiencies which centred around poor starting caused through oil drag of the plain bearings, the lack of a flywheel effect and the general problems of tending to stall coming out of a slow corner (a direct result of the engine's change from supercharged to normally aspirated form). Starting from cold was so bad, in fact, that quite often the bikes had to be towed before they would finally fire!

In the race Graham finished ninth, while West

*Works rider Jack Brett in action at Scarborough, 25 September 1952*

was 14th. However, West would have done much better if he hadn't been dramatically slowed on the first lap by clutch trouble, with his fastest lap (the fourth) being only a mere 3 seconds slower than the quickest of the race.

In the Dutch TT West was forced to retire with unspecified engine trouble, whilst in the Ulster GP the same rider finished third, and team-mate Ted Frend fifth.

The E90 Porcupine's first victory came at the first post-war BMCRC Hutchinson 100 meeting, when Frend won the 100-mile Grand Prix at a speed of 87.17 mph from George Brown (Vincent HRD) and Jack Brett (Norton).

In the 1948 Senior TT Frend, West and Graham were all retirements, whilst in the Dutch TT West finished third behind Artie Bell (Norton) and Nello Pagani (Gilera). The following weekend West improved upon this with a second in Belgium. The Ulster that year was given the title 'Grand Prix of Europe', Graham was the top placed Porcupine rider in third spot. That November a works Porcupine took a total of 18 world records at Montlhéry, on the outskirts of Paris.

In 1949 the FIM instituted the first series of classic races counting towards the newly-introduced World Championships, both for riders and constructors.

*A decade after AMC pulled out of racing, Kent dealer Tom Arter persuaded AMC to let Mike Duff (pictured left) race one of the final 1954 Porcupines. However, results were disappointing and the idea was soon abandoned*

There were a total of six races counting towards the 500 cc category. The AJS Porcupine rider Les Graham took the title with wins in Switzerland and Ulster—even though he had the disappointment of leading the Senior TT for almost the whole race but had to push in from Hillberry to finally finish tenth. Then in the Belgian GP he was forced to retire with a leaking fuel tank. Bill Doran joined the team that year and finished the season in fourth spot in the championship table, which included a highly impressive victory in Belgium.

For 1950 the AJS twin was modified with a new 6-gallon fuel tank (for longer races), redesigned oil tank, revised handlebar layout and a streamlined tail with bucket seat. There were technical changes too, including a variation in the carburettor mounting. But a blow came early in the season when Doran broke his leg in a crash during TT practice. In the race Graham finished fourth, but was generally outpaced by the newly-introduced Featherbed Nortons of

Duke, Bell and Lockett, who took the first three places.

Besides the emergence of the new, much improved Nortons, 1950 was also the year of the infamous Dunlop tyre problems—for example, the entire British works entry was forced out of the Dutch TT that year through this particular problem. Although Graham won in Switzerland and finished second in Ulster his hopes of retaining the title had gone. At the end of the year he left to join the Italian MV Agusta team.

Realizing that something had to be done the AMC development team carried out various modifications on the Porcupine that winter. These included sump lubrication, separate cylinder heads with normal finning, smaller wheels, shorter wheelbase, a new shape of fuel tank and a considerable saving in weight.

The team consisted of Bill Doran, now recovered from his Isle of Man crash the previous year, and the up-and-coming Irish star, Reg Armstrong. Although they didn't win a Grand Prix (remember it was Geoff Duke's famous Norton double year), the AJS teamsters put up a far more effective challenge gaining a trio of second places, with Doran finishing the year fourth in the championship.

The E95 version of the Porcupine appeared the following year, 1952. The designer was P. A. (Phil) Walker and he combined new with old in this first major redesign. By swinging the cylinders up from their hitherto near horizontal position to an inclination of 45 degrees he improved the cooling facilities and the line of the inlet tracts—but against this created a higher centre of gravity. Another advantage was an even shorter wheelbase. The redesigned engine, new non-loop frame and the shorter wheelbase gave the machine a totally new appearance (and in my opinion a less attractive one than the earlier model). *The Motor Cycle* described this as 'cobby'.

Because of the new engine position, Walker removed all vestiges of the 'spike' finning which had led to the machine's name. Instead, finning of the cylinders, the lower part of the heads and camshaft housing was now of conventional appearance.

Another change was that there was now chain drive to the magneto (instead of gear). There was a new rear brake, revised gearchange mechanism and new reverse-cone megaphones, the latter in an attempt to broaden the powerband. The twin Amal

*Original 1952 version of the Ike Hatch-designed 3-valve, the 7R3A*

carburettors were inclined 25 degrees to the horizontal and there was a light-alloy scoop below the tank to deflect cold air to these instruments.

The 1952 championship season couldn't have got off to a better start with AJS machines claiming first, second, and fifth places in the first 500 cc race in that year's classic series, the Swiss GP at Berne. This magnificent performance came from riders Jack Brett, Bill Doran and New Zealander Rod Coleman. This showing was not to be repeated, however, even though Bill Lomas joined the team at the TT. Robin Sherry also rode a 1951 type Porcupine at certain British short-circuit events and at the Italian GP. Sherry was also in the team when the 1953 line-up was announced the following January, together with Doran and Coleman.

There were few changes to the 499 cc twin—the major one being a new full loop frame.

Like Norton, AJS found the going even tougher as the Italian multis began to not only possess speed but much improved handling—thanks in no small part to their British riders, such as Duke and Armstrong.

In an attempt to remain competitive, the Porcupine was modified again for 1954 with a new lower frame, streamlined fuel tank and redesigned carburation system. Riders were Rod Coleman, Bob

McIntyre and Derek Farrant. But again results were hard to come by and together with Norton (now owned by AMC), AJS withdrew from racing at the end of the 1954 season.

This was not quite the end of the 'Porc' story as Glaswegian tuner Joe Potts obtained an E95 engine on loan in 1957. This was one of the final ones made and by then produced 56 bhp at 7400 rpm. But with McIntyre's Gilera contract that year the engine was eventually returned to the factory. Later still, in 1964 Tom Arter borrowed a 1954 Porcupine from the factory to use as a showroom attraction. This led to Canadian rider Duff testing the machine, but again plans to race it were shelved after Duff signed for the Japanese Yamaha concern.

## 3-valve

The 350, triple overhead-camshaft, three-valve single is perhaps the machine which today is the least known but conversely the most successful of AMC's post-war works racing efforts.

By 1951 AMC were beginning to get a mite desperate for *real* success, something which the 500 Porcupine was not able to deliver on a consistent basis. So development engineer H. J. (Ike) Hatch was given the job of rescuing AMC pride, one which was

Below
*The 7R3A 3-valve engine assembly*

AUSTRALIAN TT
1st 350 c.c. Class

SWEDISH GRAND PRIX
1st 500 c.c. Class

JUN

Above
*A works 3-valve on show at Earls Court in 1954. That year had seen the introduction of the pannier tanks on both the triple-knocker and Porcupine models*

not made any easier by a distinct lack of funds for the task in hand.

But in many ways Hatch was an ideal man for the particular task his employers had in mind, as not only was he very experienced in four-stroke engine techniques, but a recognized authority on valve-operating mechanisms.

Forced to improvise through stringent cash restraints, Hatch was left with little alternative than to consider using the production 7R as a basis. Designated the 7R3A, Hatch's new creation sported three valves—a large inlet and two smaller, radially-disposed, exhausts. However, it was the complex actuating mechanism for the valve operation which really set this engine apart. In keeping with the 7R, the inlet camshaft, set transversely across the head, was chain driven. In turn this cam transmitted a drive via spur gearing to a layshaft. Finally, bevel gears transmitted the drive from the layshaft to each of two camshafts, which lay fore-and-aft, one for each exhaust valve. A single spark plug was located just forward of the combustion chamber centre, between the exhaust valves and with a slight rearward inclination so that its business end faced the incoming mixture. The bottom half followed normal 7R practice, except for a change in the crankcase material. The unit was housed in a standard 7R with the promise of a new frame at a later date. The two-port cylinder head employed short, small diameter exhaust pipes with tiny megaphones, whilst the tacho drive was taken from the offside exhaust cam.

Compared to the 7R, the 3-valve had totally new bore and stroke measurements of 75.5 × 78 mm, giving a much shorter stroke than before. Its power output was in the region of 36 bhp at 7200 rpm (AMC never released exact details).

The design philosophy that had prompted Hatch to carry out the above modifications were all based on engineering principles of the period and it is interesting to note that some 30 years later Japanese manufacturers such as Honda used three-valve heads, but with a pair of inlet valves and a single exhaust.

As Hatch saw it the rate of heat dissipation was greater with two small exhaust valves than with one large one, this having the effect of cooling the incoming charge of petrol/air mixture and thus increasing the volumetric efficiency. The widely splayed exhaust ports also permitted an improved cooling airflow across the cylinder head and the central location of the sparking plug ensured a shorter flame travel. Another advantage of small, light exhaust valves was minimal valve float which was so often a problem in conventional two-valve racing engines.

Team leader Rod Coleman finished fourth in the 1952 world series and third in 1954 making those years successful ones for the Hatch 3-valver. The undoubted highlight was his victory in the 1954 Junior TT at an average speed of 91.51 mph with team-mate Derek Farrant in second place. This was the AJS factory's first Isle of Man victory for 24 years.

The triple-knocker's only other classic race success was the first Grand Prix of 1954 which was the French when local hero Pierre Monneret scored a highly popular win in front of his own countrymen on a 1953 machine.

Although relatively unchanged mechanically, the 3-valve was given a completely new appearance for the 1954 season, with major alterations being made to the frame and tanks and the carburation system. The frame was lowered by 1½ in. at the steering head and a massive 6½-gallon 'pannier' type tank fitted (a similar version was fitted to that year's Porcupine).

A conventional, remotely mounted float chamber was retained but a pump now delivered fuel from the tank (in which the fuel was partly below float chamber height). The pump was driven by the offside exhaust cam. By now power output was up to 40 bhp at 7800 rpm.

*During 1954 Hatch had redesigned the 3-valve, and the most significant change was to replace the cam drive chain with a shaft and bevels. Had AJS continued, the new engine, coded 7R3B, would have carried the factory's colours into 1955.*

Spurred on by the successes in the French GP and Isle of Man (the first two classics that year), designer Hatch was authorized to carry out more development work on the triple knocker. The main change in what was to emerge as the 7R3B, was the substitution of chain drive, by shaft and bevel gears. This meant that any alteration to the compression ratio could be accomplished simply by inserting shims under the cylinder barrel and varying the thickness of the Oldham couplings to adjust the length of the vertical shaft. The drive to the three camshafts was also altered slightly but the general layout remained basically unchanged.

Sadly, before serious testing of the 7R3B could take place Ike Hatch died and Jack Williams took over his place as chief development engineer.

Then in February 1955 came the announcement that AMC racing policy had changed and from now on the company (together with Norton) would concentrate its efforts on the production AJS 7R and Matchless G45 models. So together with the Porcupine the 3-valve racer was shelved. This meant that the new 7R3B was destined never to be raced in anger and so another chapter in the history of the British racing motorcycle came to a close.

# 7
# Rocket 3
# and Trident

British manufacturers had traditionally posed the only threat to Harley-Davidson and Indian at the Daytona Beach races initially, and later at the Daytona 200. Since 1937 Indian had had three Daytona victories and Harley-Davidson 16, while Norton had four wins, Triumph three and BSA one.

With the launch of the first BSA Rocket 3 and Triumph Trident 740 cc (67 × 70 mm) three-cylinder models in September 1968 the British looked set to offer a new challenge not just on the street but the race circuit too. Work on the new design had begun back in 1964 with Bert Hopwood and Doug Hele as the designers but it was not until some three years later that the pair were to receive official blessing to proceed by the BSA/Triumph hierarchy. And

*A 1970 works BSA Rocket 3, Daytona, March 1970*

then it was out of fear of what the Japanese were about to do to sales in the larger capacity sector rather than enthusiasm for the new project!

In fact, it had been Hopwood who back in 1961 had the original idea of creating a 750 class machine out of $1\frac{1}{2}$ Triumph Speed Twins. In many ways the finished product was just that with many conventional Triumph design features. The only real difference between the BSA and Triumph versions was that the BSA had the engine inclined forward 15 degrees, whilst in the Triumph it was upright.

Each employed pushrods and a one-piece crank with white metal big-ends and four main bearings. The con-rods were of light alloy whilst the camshafts followed traditional Triumph pattern, being gear-driven on the offside. Unlike the BSA and Triumph twins, the cylinder barrels were also of alloy with austenitic liners. There were three sets of contact

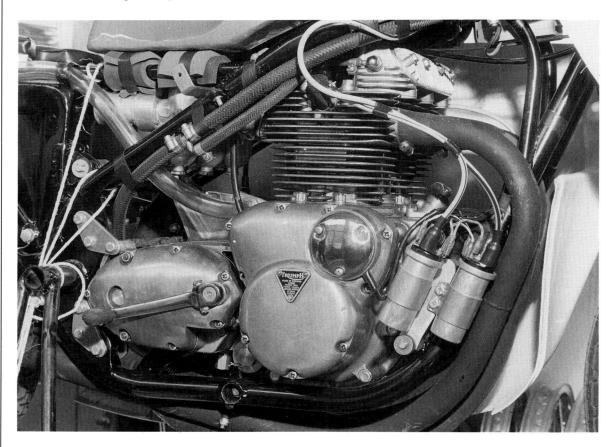

breakers which were driven off the end of the exhaust cam. Carburation—both on the roadsters and racers—was by a trio of Amal Concentric Mark 1 carburettors, but bigger instruments were used on the track bikes. Primary drive was by a triplex chain with a single-plate diaphragm clutch, designed by Doug Hele with a Borg and Beck friction plate.

The unit-construction, vertically-split crankcases housed a four-speed gearbox, but the design was of the dry sump type, with a separate oil tank. Even on the roadster there was an oil cooler as standard. Besides the inclined engine configuration, the Rocket 3 also differed in having twin downtubes, whereas the Trident had only one.

Triumph factory tester Percy Tait was the first man to race one of the 3s at a major event, when he finished sixth at the 1969 Hutchinson 100. That November the BSA/Triumph competition department was given the go-ahead to prepare pukka racing versions for the Daytona 200 the following March. In just over three months the race bikes were designed, built and tested for this major event. Whilst Doug Hele oversaw the preparation of the engine units, a totally new frame was commissioned from specialist Rob North. And right from the first

Above
*Engine details of the 1970 Triumph Trident Formula 750 racer. Note the different inclination of the cylinders in comparison to the BSA version*

Right
*The great Mike Hailwood rode for BSA at Daytona in both 1970 and 1971*

test session it was obvious that Hele and North had both done their respective tasks superbly. The bikes were both extremely quick *and* blessed with leech-like roadholding.

Once across the Atlantic this early promise was shown to be completely founded when Gene Romero set Daytona Raceway alight during the official practice sessions by being speed trapped at 165.44 mph. Romero also set the fastest qualifying lap at 157.36 mph. Not only this but the great Mike Hailwood had come out of retirement to race a BSA triple at Daytona and actually led the race at one stage.

But there was one serious problem, one that all the testing back in Britain had failed to find: the machine's distinctive 'letterbox' fairings did not allow quite enough air to reach the engine and the result in the hot Florida sun was serious overheating.

*Dick Mann receives a well-earned kiss after winning the 1971 Daytona 200 for BSA*

First Hailwood's bike was affected then Romero's. But although the Englishman was forced to retire when a valve dropped, Romero struggled on to finish second with Don Castro on another triple third. The victory went instead to Dick Mann's works Honda CB750.

But the Daytona setback was only temporary and very soon the BSA and Triumph triples were winning big races on both sides of the Atlantic. Hopwood had wanted to build a production bike more closely akin to the works racers, but unfortunately he was never authorized to proceed by the management; which must have been particularly annoying considering its undoubted sales potential with the era of the Superbike just around the corner.

The next stage in the evolution of the British challenge was the machines entered for the 1970 series of long-distance endurance races. In the Production TT Malcolm Uphill won on a Trident at 97.71 mph whilst another Trident showed the opposition the way home in the French Bol d'Or classic ridden by Paul Smart and Tom Dickie.

With Daytona still the main prize, work commenced that winter on four new racers for the 1971 season, two Rocket 3s and two Tridents, and by February details were released to the press. With the power output upped to 84 bhp at 8500 rpm the bikes were even quicker than the previous year— probably good for 170 mph on optimum gearing.

The changes included twin Lockheed hydraulically-operated discs in place of the giant Fontana double-sided drum brakes up front, a single Lockheed disc at the rear, Amal Concentric carburettors replacing the GPs from the same source, and a reduction in the Rob North frame height by some 2 in. to improve frontal penetration. All four machines had been built at Meriden under the watchful eye of Doug Hele. Riders were to be Mike Hailwood (BSA) and Paul Smart (Triumph), the other two, plus some 1970 models, to be ridden by American riders—most notably the 1970 winner Dickie Mann.

In almost a carbon copy of the 1970 race Hailwood led at Daytona until once again he was put out with valve trouble. Then Paul Smart led before his Trident cried enough with a holed piston with only 13 laps to go. It was then left to that wily old campaigner Dickie Mann to sneak yet another famous victory but this time aboard a Rocket 3. Romero repeated his 1970 result with second place on a Trident, whilst the 20-year-old Don Emde was third on another Rocket 3.

*Paul Smart in action with one of the works Trident production machines*

The Daytona success was to be just the start of a fantastic year for the BSA/Triumph 3s as they quite simply swept everything else aside.

At the Easter three-meeting, Anglo-American Match Race Series, the entire British *and* American teams were mounted on them. With the Brits beating their Stateside brothers by the convincing 183–137 scoreline, all six races were won by just two riders—Rocket 3-mounted Ray Pickrell and his Trident riding partner Paul Smart (each with three victories).

In May the triples won both the 200-mile Formula Race and 500-mile Grand Prix d'Endurance at Thruxton. Ray Pickrell took the former on a Rocket 3 with Paul Smart taking second place on a Trident. Percy Tait and Dave Croxford shared the winning Triumph 3 in the 500-miler and Bob Heath and John Barton brought a BSA version home into second spot.

The winning streak continued at the TT in June when Ray Pickrell took the Production event at 100.7 mph on a Trident, with Tony Jefferies (Trident) second and Bob Heath (Rocket 3) third. Tony Jefferies then went on to win the Formula 750 TT at 102.85 mph, Ray Pickrell coming second on a Rocket 3.

This pattern continued and at Silverstone in

*Ray Pickrell, winner of the 1972 Formula 750 TT on a Triumph triple*

August—the first international motorcycle meeting at the Northamptonshire circuit for six years—Pickrell won the 750 Production Race at 99.34 mph on a Rocket 3 whilst Smart took the Formula 750 event on a Trident at 103.4 mph, with Tait (Trident) second and Pickrell (Rocket 3) third.

September saw what to many was the most memorable success for one of the British 3s. This came with John Cooper in the saddle, when the 33-year-old Derby-born rider scored a sensational victory in the prestigious Race of the Year at Mallory Park. What made this race special was the opposition—not only his BSA and Triumph team-mates but the likes of Giacomo Agostini on the MV Agusta 500-3, Barry Sheene 500 Suzuki and Jarno Saarinen and Phil Read on Yamaha twins.

Twenty-six riders lined up for the 38-lap race and from a clutch start Agostini and Cooper shot into the lead. The Italian star led for ten laps before 'Moon-eyes' Cooper got his production-based machine ahead of the pukka race bike. On lap 14 Cooper's race nearly came to an abrupt halt when he got into a lock-to-lock slide at the Esses which resulted in Agostini regaining the lead. But Cooper had not given up the fight and to the cheers of the partisan crowd the BSA rider retook the lead once more. This time he retained it to claim the £1050 first prize.

**Above**
*Rickman-framed Trident racer, one of many successful specials housing either the BSA or Triumph triple engine unit built in the early 1970s*

**Below**
*Works riders Pickrell (far left) and Percy Tait (far right) receive an action picture of themselves from Walker Henderson, head of Shell Oil Retail at Shell-Mex House, 11 November 1971*

*Alex George with multi TT winner 'Slippery Sam', arguably the most successful Trident of them all. The pair are pictured here at Governor's Bridge during their record-breaking 102.82 mph lap in the 1975 Production event*

Cooper repeated this success abroad when he went over to North America and won the final major Stateside meeting of the year at Ontario, California on his Rocket 3. With two 125-mile legs, the race was claimed to be the richest in the world at the time.

As if this wasn't enough Cooper also beat Agostini for the second time in as many months to claim victory in the Race of the South at Brands Hatch.

But unfortunately in the very same month, October 1971, the BSA-Triumph Group were in dire financial straits. The banks had withdrawn credit facilities and the group's share dealings on the London Stock Exchange were suspended. All this couldn't have happened at a worse time for the racing effort—just as the vast empire was about to finally collapse its racing machinery was pulling off the best ever results. With such competitive bikes it seemed a tremendous shame that it all had to end.

Somehow at least part of the effort survived. For example, the Trident which Ray Pickrell took to victory in the 1972 Production TT had been rescued from a cellar and subsequently prepared in the former race shop manager's home for Pickrell to ride.

Nicknamed *Slippery Sam* it was later bought by Les Williams and got a further hat-trick of TT victories: Tony Jefferies in 1973; Mick Grant in 1974; and for the 10-lap production marathon in 1975 when it was shared by Dave Croxford and Alex George. This made an amazing *five* TT victories for *Slippery Sam*. The bike was notably quick, but it is only fair to point out that it wasn't *standard*. Its host of special goodies included 11.5 : 1 pistons, special high-lift cams, a close ratio Quaife five-speed box and a modified frame. In the braking department at first one of the massive Fontana four leading-shoe drums was used but from 1974 Lockheed twin discs were fitted. With a full fairing, special seat and tank, *Slippery Sam* weighed in at under 400 lb dry. A number of replicas were constructed by Les Williams but the original now has a permanent home at the National Motorcycle Museum near Birmingham.

With the break-up of the BSA-Triumph Group and its subsequent acquisition by NVT (Norton-Villiers-Triumph) many of the works racing triples were sold off. In addition several more works replica F750 racers were built from standard machines. So today when you visit a classic event the odds are that you will be treated to the sight *and* sound of these magnificent British racing motorcycles. In many ways the Rocket 3 and Trident were perhaps the last of the really great motorcycles made within the confines of the British Isles.

# 8
# Specials

A phenomenon of the classic British racing scene was the truly vast number of specials, many highly innovative, which sprung up in the years following the end of World War 2.

To do justice to all these would take a book in itself—so I have chosen ten examples to illustrate the diversity and technical flair which these 'privateer' engineers displayed.

The ones selected are, of course, my choice and I am absolutely certain that someone else would probably have selected a different batch. I've also tried to include the various eras: the 1950s, the 1960s and finally the 1970s. Again, some are the creations of enthusiastic motorcycle traders whilst others are truly home-spun affairs.

Sadly, lack of space has prevented many equally deserving efforts such as the large number of highly interesting racers created by Bert Fruin, which were both singles and multis—four-stroke and two-stroke, or the very rapid and successful dohc Lomas Royal Enfield—a converted pre-war 250 with which future world champion Bill Lomas achieved much of his early success. And of course not forgetting Geoff Monty's partner Allen Dudley-Ward, who created some highly interesting specials.

There were also several 'white elephants'. As an example I have included Colin Lyster's Lynton. In fact during the 1960s and early 1970s there were several, the most well known being the Read-Weslake twin, the KRM four and the infamous Manx Lottery project.

## Beasley

One of the most industrious and ingenious of the post-war British special builders was Douglas St. John Beasley of Coventry. Beasley had been a rider of considerable note in the late 1940s and early 1950s, the highlight of his career being in 1948 when he finished third in the Lightweight (250 cc) TT on an Excelsior.

He then entered the role of entrant and special builder and sponsored a variety of riders, including Cecil Sandford who won the 1954 Hutchinson 100 at Silverstone on a Beasley-Velocette.

But the most interesting, if not the most successful, of the Beasley specials was a little known double overhead-camshaft 125 which he built for the 1955 season. It was conceived as a potential challenger to the all conquering Italian Mondial and MVs and consumed something like 800 man hours to construct.

The engine featured a 55 × 56 mm bore and stroke with the camshafts being driven by an endless simplex chain from a half-time sprocket, driven from the mainshaft and pressure lubricated. Chain tension was maintained by a top idler (jockey sprocket) and 4 in. radius slippers.

This particular camshaft layout restricted the compression ratio to 9.25:1. Beasley chose to 'play safe' and use an MV piston—a marque with which

*Doug Beasley's dohc 125, circa 1956*

*Beasley's overbored, Triumph Cub-engined special at Mallory Park in 1959. It displaced 249 cc*

he had had some experience, as he owned one of the first of the single-knocker Sport Competizione 125 production racers imported into Britain during early 1953.

The cylinder barrel, machined from solid, had an austenitic liner, and the head was also machined from solid. The $4\frac{1}{2}$ in. diameter flywheels were manufactured in the same way.

The use of a Triumph Terrier crankcase was ingenious, complete with primary drive and gears for the bottom end. But Beasley had substantially uprated the main bearings in view of the extra stress which the engine would have to withstand.

Lubricated separately in standard form, the Triumph crankcase and gearbox casting were modified by drillways for unit lubrication. It was envisaged that if testing was successful then further work would be needed to construct a set of closer ratio gears—and probably a five- or even six-speed cluster.

To cope with the projected 11,500 rpm, which was a very high figure in 1955, Beasley chose to use hairpin valve-springs and a two-valve layout but realized that his biggest problem was likely to be valve bounce, even if the hairpins were changed at frequent intervals.

The chassis and running gear for the Beasley dohc 125 came from the Birmingham engineer Ernie Earles. This was identical to the one used the pre-

*Another of Doug Beasley's creations was this NSU-powered, Featherbed-framed special, which is shown with its creator in April 1960*

vious year when future World Champion Bill Lomas rode the machine to victory at Silverstone on 11 April 1954 with an MV engine inserted.

The duplex frame incorporated pivoted-fork rear suspension with adjustable Girling shocks, and was bronze-welded throughout from Reynolds 531 tubing of no more than 18 gauge. The Earles pivoted front fork was a unique design with a single, inverted U-shaped tube forming the main stanchions. This was welded to the bottom end of a single tube which lay in front of and parallel to the steering head, to which it was attached by top and bottom lugs. The main stanchion member was braced to the lower end of the steering head by another, shorter, inverted U-tube. Like the stanchions, the pivoted fork was made from Reynolds 531 tapered tubing and a pair of Woodhead-Monroe suspension units permitted a total front wheel deflection of some four inches.

On both sides of the machine streamlined pannier tanks carried the fuel and were shaped to blend with the rider's arms. An AC fuel pump, driven from the inlet camshaft, lifted the fuel from these tanks to a small header tank where it passed to the carburettor by gravity. Blending with the pannier tanks was a small fairing which extended round the steering head and carried a small perspex screen and also the front mudguard.

A rectangular oil tank sat behind the steering head which, when enclosed by the streamlining, was out of sight.

Unfortunately, after all this work the engine's performance did not live up to expectations and was soon abandoned. However, the chassis design was later used by Beasley when he built another special during the winter of 1957-8. The only real difference was a *light alloy*, instead of steel, frame.

The new engine comprised a Triumph Cub bottom end, topped by an MOV Velocette cylinder within which ran a piston from a 649 cc T110 Triumph to bring the capacity up to 246 cc. A Cub head on the Velo barrel, but reworked to provide a squish band, combustion chamber, and radiused valve seats completed the picture. The machine was ridden in several outings by the Triumph tester and later works rider, Percy Tait, achieving moderate success.

## Jones

In a story which *The Motor Cycle* ran in their 26 March 1959 issue the journal stated: 'As an exponent of the do-it-yourself cult, Dennis Jones of Long Eaton, near Nottingham, can have very, very few rivals'. Never was a statement more accurate.

Jones started his craft in the war years with a supercharged four-cylinder two-stroke, then in the early 1950s he created the JEL (Jones Earles Lomas), a 250 twin racer, and later still followed this up with another twin—this time entirely of his own handiwork.

But his real *pièce de résistance* made its public debut at Mallory Park one cold and wet day in March 1959 (hence the article in *The Motor Cycle*). This was a superbly crafted 496 cc dohc four, with square 54 × 54 mm bore and stroke dimensions.

**Above**
*The Jones 500 four, an extremely neat piece of work*

**Below**
*Engine details of the Jones four, including Scintilla magneto, Amal carburettors and Albion gearbox*

Although using the same transverse layout as an MV or Gilera, the Jones four had much more in common with his earlier twin-cylinder models. It had taken just over two years to progress from the first drawings to the Mallory Park outing.

Local motorcyclists in the Long Eaton area were no doubt given something to talk about when, with silencers fitted and registration plates mounted fore and aft, the Jones four was run in on public roads, serving its creator as ride-to-work transport while he made various adjustments to the machine.

Mounted across the frame, the Jones engine embodied a crankcase split both horizontally and on the vertical centre-line. The crankcase, therefore, comprised four parts—an arrangement adopted for ease of machining purposes as Dennis Jones' workshop was a relatively tiny affair at the rear of his home. For the same reason the cylinder heads and barrels were separate components. Of built-up construction with hardened steel crankpins pressed in the pairs of flywheels, the crankshaft was supported in no fewer than six journal roller bearings. The cylinders were numbered 1 to 4, reading from the nearside of the machine. Formed on the middle of the crank was a pinion which drove the camshafts through a train of gears running up between cylinders 2 and 3. The primary drive to the gearbox was from teeth milled into the periphery of the nearside flywheel of number 2 crank assembly. Light alloy con-rods ran directly on the crankpins.

Lubrication was by a gear type pump which first pumped oil to the main bearings and thereafter via drillways in the crank to the big-ends.

Valve included angle was 90 degrees which accounted for an unusual chisel-edge shape for the piston crowns. Inlet and exhaust valves were manufactured in KE965 steel and the short tappets were interposed between the cams and valve stems. Clearance was adjusted by fitting valve end cap shims of varying thickness.

The sparks were provided by a Scintilla Vertex magneto, which was mounted horizontally at the rear of the cylinders and driven from the cam drive gear train. Exploratory revving up to 13,000 rpm showed no particular problems.

The gearbox and clutch used some Albion components, but like the rest of the machine was largely of Dennis Jones' own manufacture.

Weighing 380 lb, the Jones four looked a well finished and purposeful mount in its blue colour scheme; and at $17\frac{1}{4}$ in., the overall width of the engine was only about $\frac{1}{2}$ in. more than that of the works Gilera.

The frame was made from Reynolds 531 tubing, and of the duplex loop type. Twin loop tubes extended side by side from the steering head to the rear of the fuel tank, where they diverged and then continued rearward to the seat extremity. The steering head was given extra reinforcement.

The telescopic front forks were home-made, whilst Woodhead Monroe rear shocks took care of the rear end. An unusual feature of the $7\frac{1}{4}$ in. brakes, which were fitted to both wheels, was that the cam spindles were coaxial with the wheel spindles.

A large capacity light alloy fuel tank held over 6 gallons, which was ample even for the longest race. The 6-pint oil tank was mounted between the frame tops, with the filler cap just ahead of the seat nose—as on later Manx Nortons.

Shortly after creating his 'four' Dennis Jones became a partner in a garage business, bearing his name, at Syston, Leicestershire. At first this specialized in two-wheels, but with the downturn in sales during the 1960s they later switched to Reliant three-wheelers.

Unfortunately, this meant that the former Rolls-Royce gunsmith had far less spare time and his four was never fully developed. However, his twins were a frequent sight at Midlands circuits, like Mallory Park, until well into the 1960s.

# LCH

Starting in 1951 at the age of 31, Leonard (Len) Clifford Harfield's first project was a sleeved down Royal Enfield 150 cc which was eventually converted to dohc—and so the first LCH special was born.

Inspired by this initial creation Harfield, a garage foreman in Southampton, soon began to plan his

*The 1953 version of Len Harfield's long-running dohc 125 special*

*Harfield with 125 LCH, 27 March 1956. The venue is Silverstone*

next project. This was to emerge in early 1954 as a particularly neat double-knocker 124.5 cc (55 × 52.5 mm) single that, except for the crankcase, which began life as part of a side-valve 250 Royal Enfield, was almost totally his own work. The choice of bore size was dictated by the need to use a stock piston (in this case a 3T Triumph). As Harfield proposed manufacturing his own crankshaft assembly, the stroke requirement offered no problem. As already mentioned RE crankcases were used. The timing side of these was modified by cutting away the oil-pump housing and welding a plate into the resultant gap. Next, the bearing housings were opened up for a ball race on the timing side and rollers for the drive. Steel flywheels were machined from a solid billet and prepared to receive $\frac{7}{8}$ in. diameter mainshafts. A 1-in. diameter case hardened crankpin completed the crank assembly—the conrod was one from a Douglas Sprite light aero engine!

The alloy cylinder barrel used a cast-iron liner, and Harfield undertook the manufacture of patterns for the head, camboxes and the two chain cases, casting all his own light-alloy components, with the exception of the cylinder head. This he found required a specialist technique and was provided by an Idoson casting, into which he fitted his own valve seats and guides to give an included angle of 84 degrees. Springs were of the hairpin variety.

The drive to the double overhead-camshafts was by chain and a train of gears. A chain connected the half-time shaft to the principal intermediate shaft above the head, this carried a pinion by which the drive was transmitted through intermediates to the camshaft. The valves were manufactured in KE765 and KE965 steels for the inlet and exhaust respectively, the cams operating directly on hardened tappets with the adjustment by shims.

The sparks were provided by a BTH TT magneto, which was driven by a chain from a second sprocket on the half-time shaft. Lubrication was of the dry sump type.

The transmission was taken care of by an Albion HJ close-ratio gearbox, which was mounted between extensions of the dural engine plates.

Like so many British special builders of the

period, Harfield chose to construct his frame on similar lines to the famous Featherbed Norton chassis. The main frame had tubes of $\frac{3}{4}$ in. × 16 gauge, in T45 aircraft quality steel.

The suspension was taken care of by a pair of Earles type forks (although at first AMC teledraulics were fitted), whilst at the rear there were a pair of modified Newton car-type shock absorbers.

The finished product was only the first of several LCH specials over the next decade, all of which displayed these same purposeful lines.

For example, a totally new 125 cc twin overhead-camshaft power unit was produced in 1957. This time it had a set of 250 cc Rudge crankcases with much modified flywheels—from 75-ton steel. Mainshafts were from EN36, while the whole assembly was supported by four roller main bearings. The bore and stroke were also changed from the earlier type engine at 53 × 56 mm, giving 124.8 cc. The cylinder head was part-spherical, with the spark plug mounted centrally.

Lever type cam followers were used, operating direct between the camshafts and the valves and caps. Hairpin valve springs were enclosed in wells cast in the cylinder head, whilst separate camboxes each housed a camshaft and lever.

*Len Harfield in action during the 1956 Ultra Lightweight TT*

Drive for the Smiths rev-counter came from the camshaft, whilst the drive to the camshaft was by now by spur gears. These gears were mounted on ball races and two of them were adjustable for mesh to enable a change in the compression ratio to be made. Ignition was now by battery/coil.

A new frame was constructed for 1958 which weighed in at only 11 lb. This was a saving of almost half from the previous year and not only this but overall height was also reduced. Further weight pruning had come from redesigned engine mountings and liberal drilling of the rear hub assembly and by use of light alloy for the oil tank. In total a weight reduction of 50 lb was made, so the LCH now tipped the scales at an impressively low 207 lb dry.

In the quest for more power a new cylinder head, featuring larger valves, was made and later that year Harfield modified this to take twin plugs.

The following year saw more changes but this time restricted entirely to the engine and gearbox, the latter being a new type of lightweight Albion.

The various 125 LCH specials made five Isle of Man TT appearances. In 1955 Harfield was eighth and last 'official' finisher, and in 1958 and 1959 was credited with 16th. In 1956, the Southampton rider/ engineer was adjudged 'NF' (non finisher) and finally in 1957 he retired on lap 3.

After the arrival of the first dohc Ducati Grand Prix and later the two-stroke Bultaco, machines like

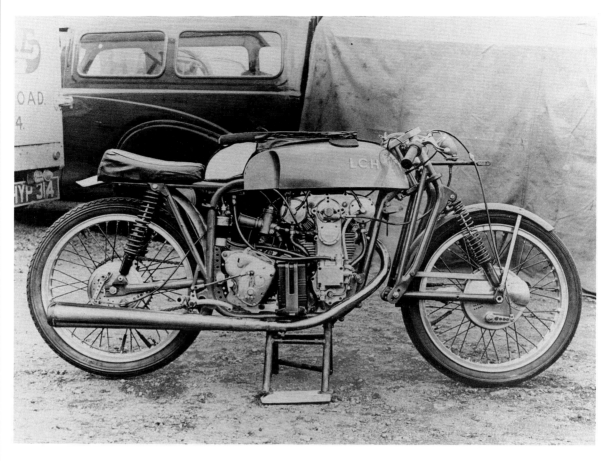

*By 1959 the LCH looked like this, neat and aggressive in every line*

Len Harfield's LCH were totally outclassed. However, rather than simply throw in the towel he then built himself an extremely neat racer powered by a Honda CB72 twin-cylinder engine. Housed in familiar LCH cycle parts this made its debut in 1963 to become the final creation of L. C. Harfield.

## LEF

The initials LEF stood for Lewis, Ellis and Foster, who ran a motorcycle workshop in Watford, Hertfordshire during the immediate post-war period. Their first attempt at building a racing motorcycle of their own design came in the late 1940s, when D. W. J. Harrowell rode a beautifully prepared 248 cc twin-cylinder LEF at various southern circuits during 1948, 1949 and 1950, including appearances at the TT in the two later years.

But their supreme effort came later with a superbly crafted double-knocker 125. This emerged in time for the 1954 season and was a particularly neat piece of work. And as *The Motor Cycle* put it:

'the machine has an appearance which would not disgrace a factory product'.

The bore and stroke of the engine were $55 \times 52.5$ mm, which gave 124 cc. Rigidity and ample bearing dimensions were a feature of this most interesting creation. The complete crankshaft comprising mainshafts, flywheels and crankpin, was manufactured from a solid 7-in. diameter billet of 40-ton steel. This construction meant a split big-end with Vandervell shells.

The full skirt three-ring piston was steeply domed and had a compression ratio of 9.5:1. This ran in a Wellworthy Alfin cylinder, with replaceable austenitic liner.

Of bi-metal construction, the cylinder-head comprised a bronze skull with cast-on light alloy shell. The included angle of the valves was 90 degrees. The inlet port had a 5-degree downdraught and both ports were slightly offset to the longitudinal axis of the machine. Carburation was taken care of by an Amal 15TT with $\frac{7}{8}$ in. bore.

There were two separate cam boxes and the cams themselves were supported in the two ball races. An unusual feature of the design was that both gears and chains were used in the camshaft drive. Another feature was that an extremely fine vernier adjustment of the valve timing was possible—a variation of one tooth on a chain sprocket and three teeth on the corresponding gear altered the timing by less than one degree of crankshaft rotation. A flange fitting BTH racing magneto was gear-driven from the rear combined gear.

Lubrication was taken care of by a Norton gear pump, driven from a worm gear on the end of the timing-side mainshaft and the off-side end of the camshaft drove a timed engine breather.

Power was transmitted via an Albion four-speed box with close ratios and chains were employed for both the primary and final rear drive.

The frame was of the full duplex cradle type and either bronze welded or bolted up, and a pair of Francis Barnett shock absorbers were used at the rear.

Steering head bearings were of the Timken taper roller type and Metal Profiles supplied the telescopic front forks, the dual drum front stopper was from

*LEF dohc 125 engine, April 1954*

*John Harrowell in action with the twin-cylinder LEF 250 during the Lightweight TT, 1950*

the same source. The rear brake hub was from a Matchless and both hubs were laced to 19 in. Dunlop alloy rims.

The alloy Lyta petrol and oil tanks, with capacities of 2½ gallons and 4 pints respectively, were rubber mounted.

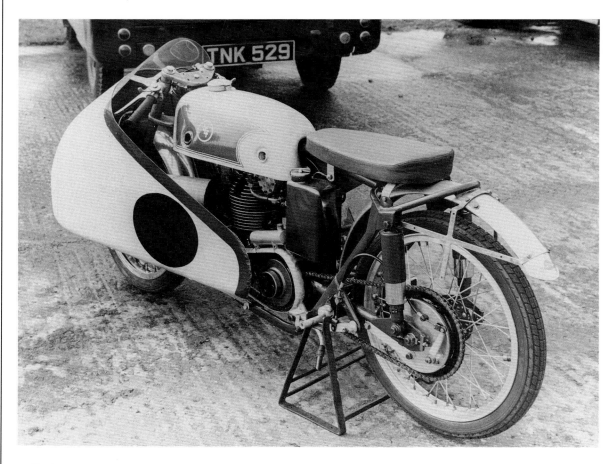

*Fully-faired LEF 125 at Silverstone, April 1956*

The power output of 12 bhp at 9500 rpm provided a maximum speed of over 80 mph, which for its time was quite rapid.

Without doubt the highlight of the 125LEF's racing career came at the 1956 TT when Dave Chadwick piloted it into fifth place in the Ultra Lightweight event, held over the shorter Clypse circuit, at an average speed of 60.25 mph. The LEF with Chadwick aboard had the satisfaction of not only finishing in front of privately-entered FB Mondials and MV Agusta machinery, but the Czech CZ works rider Parus. Like the majority of the machines in the race, the LEF wore a fully streamlined 'dustbin' fairing.

Both the earlier 250 twin and the dohc 125 single have survived and were paraded at the CRMC (Classic Racing Motorcycle Club) 'Classicfest' at Donington Park in July 1987.

## Lyster

Rhodesian Colin Lyster left his Bulawayo home in 1961 to race in Europe but after four seasons of racing, mainly on the Continent, Lyster switched to the manufacture of frames and disc brakes for other riders.

By late 1966, with his racing components having quickly made a name, Lyster decided to branch out into a new role, that of motorcycle manufacturer. This was at a time when the British racing singles had been out of production for almost four years and spares were getting expensive—if you could find them.

Lyster could see a ready market for an easy-to-service and cheap replacement power unit, but how could he build it at the right price? The answer came the following year when he started work on the design of the Lynton. This was a 60 bhp, 499 cc watercooled parallel twin. The plan called for a bore and stroke of 72.65 × 60.4 mm with four valves per cylinder and two overhead camshafts. Maximum rpm was a planned 10,000. Those revs represented a mean piston speed of 4000 ft/min. But his first prototype was restricted to sohc and two valve heads.

The development costs and time schedule were helped by the fact that except for the cylinder head, pistons and a few other parts, the new engine was virtually the rear half of a 998 cc Hillman Rallye Imp car engine, itself descended from the successful Coventry Climax FWA racing unit of ten years earlier.

On the first prototype Lynton engine, the opening left by halving the Imp's aluminium alloy cylinder block-cum-crankcase casting was filled by a duralumin sheet welded on by the Argonarc process.

It was intended that on production engines, this would be a light alloy casting, attached by screws and Araldite adhesive and housing the drive-side crankshaft oil seal.

Bench tests on the prototype were done with a sawn-off Imp crankshaft, to which the outside flywheel and sprocket were attached by three dowels and a large bolt.

The pistons moved in opposite directions giving a superior primary balance and reducing pumping losses by keeping the crankcase volume constant. Firing intervals were 180 and 540 degrees alternatively, as on the Honda CB450.

On the production model a special Laystall crankshaft was planned to be used, which would be more suitable for five-figure engine speeds and provide more scope for flywheel and sprocket attachment.

Standard Imp con-rods were used but appreciably lightened by the removal of excess metal from the ends and highly polished all over. Big-end bearings were the standard split shell white metal components.

The Imp flat-crown pistons used for the initial tests were soon replaced by German Mahle forged type with a crown similar to the one on the works Hondas and other four-valve engines. Compression ratio was to have been 10:1. Valve closure was effected by duplex Terry coil springs and the camshafts came from Tom Somerton.

Drive to these camshafts was by two-stage chain. The first stage coupled a sprocket on the crankshaft to an intermediate shaft in the cylinder head. The second followed a triangular path around a sprocket on the intermediate shaft and similar sprockets on the camshaft ends.

Adjustment of the upper chain was provided by an eccentric mounting for the intermediate shaft — with a fibre rubbing strip damping out flutter on the top run. A spring-loaded blade on the slack run automatically tensioned the lower chain.

Outboard of the camshaft drive sprocket on the crankshaft was a worm wheel driving the shaft of the oil pump. Oil was delivered to the engine through a filter on the front of the cylinder block and returned to the sump by gravity. Pressure was 60 psi.

The upper end of the pump shaft drove the contact breaker for the battery/coil ignition.

*Colin Lyster's 350 Norton special, April 1966*

*The Lynton engine—essentially, it was half of a Hillman Imp Rallye car unit*

Water circulation was by thermo-syphon; but it was considered that an impellor might prove desirable and could readily be mounted on the generator bracket and driven from the offside end of the crankshaft. There were two radiators.

Separate carburettors were not used, instead both cylinders were fed by a Weber twin-choke 40DCOE instrument with built-in float chamber.

It was envisaged that many potential purchasers would want to install the engine in their own chassis but for those who didn't have a suitable frame Lyster planned to offer a complete machine (with disc brakes and Ceriani front forks) at £700–750, with the engine alone selling for £325.

Lyster's business partner in the Lynton project was Paul Brothers, who provided the financial backing for its development and the enterprise was based at a garage in Fortis Green, London N2.

The first complete Lynton machine, now using a double overhead-camshaft head, was completed just prior to the TT in May 1968. This was tested by the South African rider Errol Cowan. But 'a lack of spare engine and cam chain trouble' was cited by Lyster as the reason it was prevented from making its debut in the Senior TT.

Several proposed dates for the Lynton's debut came and went during 1968. By the time an engine was displayed at the Racing Car Show at Olympia in January 1969, Paul Brothers, attending in the absence of Colin Lyster who was ill with kidney trouble, said he had received numerous enquiries from foreign buyers. Brothers commented, 'We've changed to a single radiator and we have altered the frame layout a little'.

But the project was doomed to failure when Lyster switched his efforts into building a Honda twin-based 500, which was essentially a CB450 bot-

*Testing the 500 Lynton twin, 1968*

*Marsh 500 four-cylinder engine, 1963*

# Marsh

While the combined might of Britain's motorcycle industry largely failed to produce exotic multi-cylindered racing machines, it is a cheerful consolation that several enthusiastic engineers working from home did manage to come up with the goods. And none more so than Fred Marsh who was a fitter and turner with Harland and Wolff in his native Southampton before retiring in the late 1960s. Not only did Fred create his own four-cylinder 500, but most incredibly of all a double overhead-camshaft V8!

Born in 1901, Fred Marsh started his motor-cycling career in 1923, on an Indian. Later he changed to Ariel Square Fours, owning a total of five—three after World War 2. A keen racing enthusiast, his original inspiration to become a special builder came from the emergence in the immediate post-war period of the Italian multi-cylinder Gilera and MV Agusta four-cylinder racers.

He started his plans in 1951, but working in his spare time and with strictly limited financial resources his first machine, a dohc 496 cc (54 × 54 mm) across-the-frame four, was not finally completed until a decade later.

The layout of the engine followed that of the previously mentioned Italian fours, with the cylinders

tom half with the capacity stepped up to 496 cc by using special liners and topped by a brand new dohc head. With a minimum of finning, the head featured a four valve per cylinder layout and the camshafts, designed by Lyster, had cam profiles from the ill-fated Lynton.

This project had hardly got off the ground, however, when Lyster was taken more seriously ill with a recurrence of kidney trouble which meant the end of yet another interesing project.

*Marsh four (David Dixon) and Manx Norton (Tony Godfrey) try out at Thruxton, summer 1963*

*Carcano's Guzzi V8 inspired Southampton engineer Fred Marsh to build his own version*

inclined forward at an angle of 25 degrees and to keep the cost down as many standard production components as possible were used.

In an article in *The Motor Cycle* dated 22 February 1962, Marsh reckoned the entire project had cost around £200, plus several hundred man-hours of hard work. This was only possible because production cylinder heads (Triumph Terrier) could be modified and were readily obtainable on the second-hand market. A local firm made the crankcase castings from Marsh's patterns, and the crankshaft and con-rods presented no problems to a turner and fitter of his experience. A specialized engineering firm were able to supply pistons and cylinder, so with his modified Terrier cylinder heads the essentials of the motor were under way.

Important differences between the Marsh design and the Italian multis concerned the camshaft and primary drives. Marsh decided that taking the drive from the middle of the crankshaft and up between the inner pair of cylinders was too complicated and costly for his resources. So he opted for chain drive to the camshafts from the offside end of the crank-

shaft. The primary drive was taken off the other end of the crankshaft to a Norton clutch and gearbox.

Another reason why Fred Marsh had been keen to use the Triumph Terrier heads was that the included valve angle was 75 degrees which was almost identical to the 125 MV Agusta production racer. So, rather than experiment with his own cam design he decided to copy the MV profile.

If all this sounds like an easy operation, just consider that six months' hard effort alone was put into producing the con-rods. These were machined from solid billets of KE805 steel and were double webbed at both top and bottom for extra strength.

When finally completed the engine assembly was grafted into a Douglas Dragonfly frame which was obtained new for just £5! Other cycle parts included Ariel telescopic front forks, an ex-Derek Minter Oldani front brake and Woodhead Monroe rear shocks.

When he had finished the project in 1962, Marsh said that the bike had been built for his own pleasure rather than as a competitive race winner. Even so, short-circuit star Tony Godfrey gave it a gallop around the local Thruxton circuit.

*Fred Marsh and his 500 V8, June 1972*

And unlike certain other privately-built models, the Marsh four proved relatively trouble-free, even though it was not particularly fast.

But if the four was a tremendous achievement, the machine which followed it was truly amazing. Indeed, Fred Marsh stunned enthusiasts and professional engineers alike when in 1970 he showed off his latest creation—a mind-blowing 500 cc V8!

Like the earlier four, the 'eight' was built in his garden shed with largely home-made tools and by this time he was drawing his old age pension.

Fit and active from his long years as a marine engineer in the Southampton dockyard when he worked on such famous ships as the Queen Mary and Queen Elizabeth, Marsh spent his time working at full speed on the eight-cylinder project for some three years (1967–1970). Although he refused to put a value on it, a figure of 3000 hours of work was quoted. . . .

Once more the idea had come from the Italians, this time from when he had first heard about the existence of the legendary Guzzi V8 in 1955. So Marsh planned his engine around the Mandello

*Tommy Robb (49) with the GMS leads Mike Hailwood (20) on the Mondial at the Aintree International, 26 September 1959*

masterpiece except that he opted for air, rather than watercooling, on cost grounds.

He started with the crankshaft as he felt that this would entail the greatest amount of problems from an engineering stand point and unless these could be solved it would be pointless continuing.

The Marsh crankshaft was built up from eight separate discs of high-tensile steel $3\frac{1}{4}$ in. in diameter. He later recalled, 'It did prove a great deal of trouble—and I was on the point of giving up several times, especially when a machining operation went wrong and ruined six months' work'.

The crankshaft was lubricated by a Velocette gear type pump, but the usual scavenge duct was reversed and provided the main feed supply. The second feed outlet was used to lubricate the double overhead-camshaft valve gear. An additional feed to the big-ends was provided by scoops on the con-rod eyes which dipped into the wet sump as the crankshaft rotated.

The 480 cc (42 × 44 mm) capacity allowed the provision of reboring without going over the 500 cc limit.

An example of Fred Marsh's expertise (and patience!) was that before he could produce the 16-lobe camshaft, he had to make his own cam-grinding machine, which in turn was operated by a 5 in. lathe

*GMS without its fairing. Engine was based around a sleeved-down Gold Star unit*

of his own creation. The four camshafts were driven by a separate chain for each bank of cylinders and were arranged in a similar manner to the Coventry Climax Formula 1 car of the 1960s.

Several components were of Honda origin, including the pistons and cylinder heads from the model C105.

Surprisingly, it was the drive and carburation, rather than the engine assembly, which caused the major problems. Not only was it a case of finding eight carburettors which would do the task at hand, but also float chambers to suit both banks of cylinders.

However, it was the transmission which was to prove the most difficult. For a start, cost prevented the design being a full unit-construction layout. So the primary drive was by pinion, through an idler, to a counter shaft which transmitted the power (estimated to be around 70 bhp at 13,000 rpm) to a four-speed Norton gearbox and clutch by sprocket and chain. This ran at engine speed. The object of the idler pinion was solely to allow the engine to run forward. Marsh commented, 'Obviously I would

have preferred to have built it as a unit-construction job, taking the power from the centre of the crankshaft, passing it straight into the gearbox. But it just wasn't possible with my facilities'.

Guzzi practice showed in the home-produced frame, which like its more famous counterpart had a massive top backbone tube. From this the engine was supported by widely splayed front downtubes running from the steering head to each side of the transversely mounted 90-degree V8 engine.

The front forks and both wheels came from a Manx Norton, with Girling racing shocks at the rear.

Sadly, Fred Marsh died a few years ago but not before creating Britain's first dohc V8 motorcycle engine and this, together with his four (which still survives intact), is a lasting testament to a truly gifted engineer.

## Monty

Geoff Monty was born in Colombo, Ceylon (now Sri Lanka) in March 1917. His father was a tea planter who had built up an estate of considerable size.

Geoff came to England when he was ten and went to work at a garage four years later. Without an apprenticeship this meant doing any odd job that came along at first. Yet even so within six months

Above
*The 649 cc-engined Monard—there was also a 498 cc version. Cycle parts were based on the successful 250 GMS, so both twins had a good power-to-weight ratio*

Left
*Geoff Monty gives instructions to his rider, Bill Ivy, with the Monard twin, Mallory Park, 1964*

he was able to do the work of a skilled mechanic, which included complete stripdowns and rebuilds of car engines, gearboxes and rear axles.

The garage work—always on cars—kept him in full-time employment until 1939. During that period, though, a number of motorcycles passed through his hands as well. By this time he had entered the garage business in his own right.

With the outbreak of war Monty volunteered for service in the RAF but just prior to his entry he was invited to join Thornycrofts as an installation engineer on motor torpedo boats. He soon found the job to his liking as every conceivable type of engineering work was involved. Monty had also become interested in motorcycles, first with an HRD 500 single and later an Excelsior Manxman.

During the final stages of the war he met his future business partner, Allen Dudley-Ward. The first of the Monty specials appeared soon after the end of hostilities. This was a souped up Triumph

Tiger 100 of 1939 vintage to which Geoff fitted a pair of telescopic forks, whilst the engine was tuned and fitted with a supercharger—using a cabin compressor from a Messerschmitt BF 109 fighter.

Ridden by Monty at Blandford it proved faster than the recently introduced Triumph Grand Prix racers. But afterwards supercharging was banned, and that was the end of that particular Monty machine. But if nothing else it did whet the appetite for more track combat and acted as a prototype for the Monty and Ward pivoted rear fork and their own suspension units. During the late 1940s, together with the similar McCandless system, the swinging-arm conversion became all the rage, both for road and track.

By now Monty and Dudley-Ward had formed a business partnership, but this didn't stop the pair from becoming involved in the S P O R T (Surrey Private Owner's Racing Team) Équipe. Besides our two heroes this also comprised Harry Bostock and Phil Webb.

At the time, in 1952, Geoff Monty's mount was a heavily modified AJS 7R, with a lightweight frame of his own design.

By 1954 the Monty-Ward partnership was in full swing (which didn't stop either partner racing abroad, notably in Finland and Sweden). It was also

*The original Allen/REG prototype, circa 1949*

in 1954 that the GMV (Geoff Monty Velocette) first appeared. This was quick enough to challenge the rapid Guzzi singles of Cecil Sandford and Arthur Wheeler at the Silverstone Hutchinson 100 meeting that year. The machine was destined to become the fastest British 250 over the next couple of seasons.

The engine of the GMV was essentially a cut-down 348 cc KTT Mark VIII. The bore was left unaltered at 74 mm and the stroke reduced to 55 mm. Amazingly, the con-rod was shortened by cutting and welding! The magneto was replaced by battery/coil ignition. Other Monty modifications included a Manx Norton-type duplex frame and a major weight pruning exercise.

But if the GMV was an excellent piece of special builder's craft, the machine which followed it was even better. This was the GMS (Geoff Monty Special) which was built in the winter of 1955–6.

The new machine's heart originated from a 348 cc BSA Gold Star engine. At 71 mm the bore was considerably up on the stroke and was dictated by the use of a barrel, head and piston from the 350,

appropriately modified. To keep things within the 250 cc limit the special one-piece crankshaft had a stroke of 63 mm. Thus the capacity computed out to be 249 cc. (Later, a shorter stroke 72 × 61 mm, 247 cc engine was built.)

To reduce oil drag no internal flywheel was employed. Instead, an 8 in. diameter outside flywheel was splined to the drive-side mainshaft inboard of the engine sprocket. The valve gear was almost standard, but Monty's expertise in welding and grinding were shown in the layout of the inlet port with an unusually steep downdraught and larger throat. Initial power output was a healthy 32 bhp at 8300 rpm. In this area Monty readily acknowledged the valuable assistance of the man then in charge of Gold Star development at BSA's Small Heath factory, Roland Pike. (Pike himself had been a special builder of considerable note in the late 1940s.)

Mounted in a lightweight chassis with Manx Norton forks and brakes, the combination of Geoff Monty and the GMS proved hard to beat in the cut and thrust of British short circuits during the period 1956–8.

For 1959, Geoff decided to hang up his leathers and obtain the services of a rider for his bike—so Ulsterman Tommy Robb found himself signed up. However, Robb was not the first person to ride the GMS, as Mike O'Rourke had ridden the machine to 11th spot in the 1958 Lightweight TT. But it was during 1959 that the results really came with Robb winning at several short circuits, the 250 cc class of the North West 200 and a couple of highly impressive fourth places in the TT and Ulster GP. Later, Alan Shepherd also made his mark on the GMS.

From 1962 onwards, however, foreign manufacturers began to offer affordable production racers— Aermacchi and Bultaco, for example, and the even less expensive British two-stroke production racers such as Greeves and Cotton appeared on the scene. And so the fortunes of the GMS as a competitive racer dwindled rapidly. This coincided with the demise of the larger British four-stroke singles: the Manx Norton AJS 7R and Matchless G50. Then Geoff Monty turned his attentions to the larger classes.

The result of this was to be the Monard which put in some creditable performances during 1964, piloted by the up and coming Bill Ivy. Powered by tuned Triumph vertical twin engines of either 498 cc or 649 cc, the Monard was essentially the GMS concept with a Triumph twin, in place of a BSA single power unit.

But it was the Gold Star-based 250 which will always be associated with the Monty name, as one of Britain's most successful 250s during the late 1950s.

## REG

If success of the special builder's art is judged by the calibre of the riders who have graced its racing seat, there can only be one winner, the REG twin.

The story of this most famous of all British specials began back in 1948 when, 12 years after the last win by a British machine in the 250 cc Lightweight TT, a letter appeared in the BMCRC (British Motor Cycle Racing Club) 'Bemsee' club magazine. It suggested a consortium of interested and qualified parties to enable Britain to get a hold on the quarter-litre ladder in international racing again.

In Croydon, South London, Bob Geeson, a long-time Bemsee member and pre-war competitor at Brooklands, Donington and the Manx Grand Prix, read the letter with interest. This brought him into contact with toolmaker Gordon Allen, who was as it happened already well advanced with the construction of a prototype 250 parallel twin. But up to that time Allen's efforts had been directed

*Creator/rider Bob Geeson descending Bray Hill on his REG twin during the 1953 Lightweight TT*

towards the bottom end, and he hadn't given much thought to the top end, let alone the chassis.

The result was that Allen and Geeson decided to pool their talents and in the very short space of only 3½ months the pair conceived a racing 250 called the Allen-REG. The frame and cycle parts were all the work of Geeson—many coming from the REG Rudge single which its creator had ridden during 1948, including the Hutchinson 100 and the Manx GP.

The engine, with its 54 × 54 mm (249 cc) bore and stroke, all-alloy construction, gear-driven, double overhead camshafts, roller big-ends and three bearing crankshaft, was as the name implied, part Allen and part Geeson.

If the results obtained during 1949 by the Allen-REG—three starts and three retirements—with seized big-ends, were anything to go by Bob Geeson

should have called it a day there and then. But of course he didn't. During the winter of 1949-50 Geeson took over sole responsibility for the project, now renamed REG. The main differences of the subsequent engine redesign were at the bottom end; Allen's built-up crank was thrown out to be replaced by a one-piece Nitralloy assembly machined from solid and supported on lipped roller bearings at each end and a plain centre bearing; the seizure prone roller big-ends went overboard too, new Hiduminium con-rods running direct on the crankpins. The valve gear and its drive train had displayed weaknesses during 1949 and were likewise modified.

Like later models, the first pure REG which appeared in 1950 was almost, but not entirely, the work of Bob Geeson. However, not one to hog all the limelight, he also gave credit to receiving valuable assistance from Edgar Buckingham and Roger Ajax—all three worked for the Metal Box Company—Geeson a senior engineer designing and developing highly complex production machinery. Unfortunately, Ajax was to meet his death in a road accident during 1952.

Left
*John Surtees taking the REG to victory at Silverstone in April 1954. That year the combination was almost unbeatable on British short circuits*

Below
*REG dohc 249 cc engine, January 1954*

Other technical details included camshaft drive by six spur gears, each supported on both sides by ball bearings, thus reducing friction to the minimum.

The oil pump was driven from the timing chain and lubricant for the dry sump system was fed under pressure to both camboxes. Oil was pumped through the hollow crankshaft to a point midway between the big-end journals, from which an oilway led to each big-end. Both bearings were thus assured of an equal supply of lubricant.

Con-rods were RR56 forgings and ran direct on the crankshaft. The small-ends were unbushed. An outside flywheel was employed. Crankcase and timing-case castings were of magnesium. Ignition was by magneto.

Although the initial REG engine design was completed in January 1950, the complete machine was not ready until the later stages of TT practice that June. As a result of various problems with the cycle parts, only three practice laps were completed but, in the race itself, Geeson finished 12th after losing 16 minutes as a result of a broken oil pipe.

The remainder of that season and the following year brought their quota of teething problems but reasonable reliability seemed to be established and several promising results were achieved, including seventh place in the Ulster GP and a fine second place to Maurice Cann's Guzzi at Boreham. Redesigned valve gear gave the promise of even better results in 1952, but persistent magneto problems didn't help. Even a temporary change to coil ignition didn't prove a cure.

With the ignition problems finally solved the REG was entered for the 1953 Lightweight TT, the result was a creditable tenth spot at an average speed of 71.74 mph. From then on things began to look up. John Surtees' services were acquired as a rider—Bob Geeson had finally decided to let someone else do the riding as up to then he had not only been the designer/mechanic but also the pilot! At Blandford in August Surtees rode the REG into third place in the 250 cc final behind the Moto Guzzis of Fergus Anderson and Maurice Cann.

Subsequently, further valve-gear modifications added an extra 5 mph to the maximum velocity and later in the season Surtees took the REG to a sensational victory in the 250 cc race at the big end-of-season Brands Hatch Championship meeting in October 1953. Not only this, but the future world champion demonstrated the potential of the home-built twin by establishing lap and race records for the class.

*B. W. T. Rood leads John Surtees at Brands Hatch in the 250 cc race, 16 April 1954*

The highlights for Bob Geeson's special were in 1954. With Surtees aboard, the REG scored 15 firsts (plus another victory by Bob himself). In addition, no fewer than seven times, the Surtees/REG combination also set new race and lap records! At the

end of the season the original machine was sold to the Australian Jack Walters.

The next year, 1955, was devoted entirely to manufacturing sets of parts for two more complete bikes, one of which Geeson assembled as soon as it was ready, which was in the following summer, when it made its debut with Jim Baughn in the saddle.

But it wasn't to be for almost another three years that circumstances permitted the simultaneous operation of both REGs.

Experimentally, during 1958, a switch was made to coil ignition then, after a season back with the magnetos, Geeson adopted twin-plug ignition. But this dual ignition experiment was not a success and, in combination with certain other factors, led to a

*Rood's homebuilt double-knocker Velocette engine, spring 1954*

spate of stripped timing gears.

It was around this time that Derek Minter rode the REG to a number of victories, notably at Brands Hatch. Other riders included Arthur Wheeler (1956), John Hartle and Jack Brett (1957), Bob Anderson (1959), 'Ginger' Payne (1959–61), Norman Surtees (1960), Syd Mizen (1960–1), Ray Fay (1961) and Fred Hardy (1961–2).

With the other riders mentioned this array of riding talent was far in excess of any other British special, and so acts as a living proof to the claim that Bob Geeson's REG twin was the premier home-spun racer of the post-war era.

## Rood

B. W. T. (Benny) Rood's early racing experience came on a Mark VIII KTT Velocette, a 248 cc Mead Special of the same make, a 7R AJS, and 499 cc Manx Norton. Perhaps, not surprisingly, he formed certain views as to the various virtues of these thoroughbreds and, having at his disposal a well-equipped machine shop and various useful connections,

decided to embark on the construction of a special, conforming to his own ideas. The result was arguably one of the very top privately-owned 250s in Britain during the early 1950s.

Benny Rood's initial effort, which first appeared in 1952, was based around a KTT Velo. He had been most impressed by the performance of his original Mead-Velocette engine and so decided to build his own engine on similar lines.

In fact this first engine used a Mead-machined KTT cylinder head. Under this was a Wellworthy Alfin barrel. The latter was supplied in a raw 'as cast' form, which allowed Rood to machine the fins from solid and bore the liner to 68 mm.

A standard KTT crankcase housed specially machined flywheels of which the mainshafts were forged integrally with the flywheel discs, with a stroke of 68.5 mm the capacity was 249 cc.

The con-rod was machined from a steel forging and incorporated a strengthening rib around the big-end eye. A two-piece crankpin—a hardened and ground sleeve pressed to a tough core—was also the work of Rood himself and carried an MSS Velocette cage housing 18 rollers. Other home-made components included the camshaft and piston.

The engine lubrication followed works Velocette practice with its two scavenge pumps. With a large $1\frac{5}{32}$ in. Amal 10TT carburettor the Rood Velo peaked at 8500 rpm and was the match for almost every other privately-owned machine of its era, except for the super quick Guzzi of Maurice Cann.

The frame appeared to be a full duplex affair but actually employed a single top tube and the balance of the running gear came from a variety of sources, including Matchless (forks), BSA (fork springs) and Velocette (wheels).

During 1953 Rood scored a number of impressive wins at Crystal Palace, Silverstone and Snetterton, but even so he didn't rest on his laurels. And during the winter of 1953-4 he set about making a new cylinder head with twin camshaft valve gear, since he considered that this arrangement would give him more scope for further development.

The new head was a Y-alloy casting. Austenitic iron valve seats were shrunk in. The guides were made from Barronia, a special bronze. The included valve angle was unchanged at 70 degrees but the

*The amazing Roland Peck special, 1953*

downward inclination of the inlet port had been increased to 20 degrees.

The two-piece cambox was divided vertically in a fore-and-aft plane and to the offside of the cambox assembly was a standard KTT upper bevel box.

Driven from the timing-side mainshaft by standard KTT bevel gear train and vertical shaft, the crown wheel was bolted to a flanged shaft which was supported in a double-row ball race in the bevel box and roller race in the cambox cover. Keyed to this shaft and secured by a nut was the middle pinion of the cambox gear train.

Interposed between this pinion and the camshaft pinions were two idler gears. Pressed into the bore of each of these gears was a hardened sleeve, supported by a double row of caged rollers running on a hardened spindle. The offside ends of the spindles were a press fit in the cambox, while the nearside ends were threaded internally to receive bolts which clamped the spindles against the inside face of the cambox cover.

Each camshaft was supported by a ball bearing on the timing side and roller bearing in the cambox cover. The hollow tappets were made of case

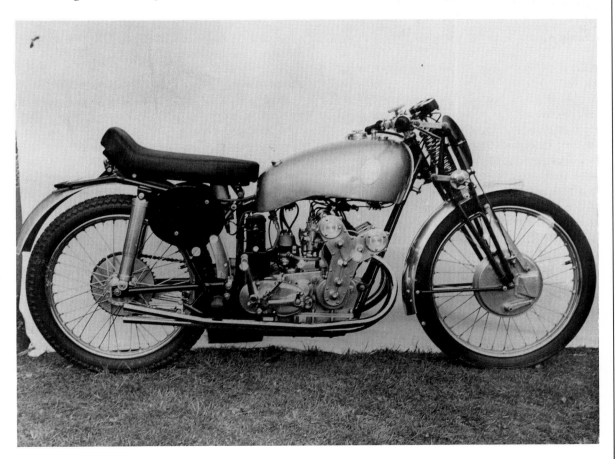

*RP 250 four-cylinder engine for the world to see*

hardened EN39 steel, and adjustment was carried out by shims. To prevent the tappets from rotating in their phosphor-bronze guides, a flat was ground on the side of each tappet for a portion of its length which engaged with the end of a hardened pin protruding through the guide.

Lubrication was effected by jets of oil directed to the contact points of cams and tappets. From a trough beneath each cam, a small bore pipe took oil to each valve guide. Oil drained from a well in the cambox to the lower bevel housing, from where it was pumped back to the tank.

The size of the carburettor remained unchanged, in fact the only other modification was a new alloy fuel tank which was needed as the original did not have enough clearance for the cambox. Testing showed that maximum revs had climbed to 9000 rpm, with particularly clean pick-up above 4500 rpm.

Benny Rood never raced his double-knocker Velocette special in the TT and his original sohc version retired in the 1953 Lightweight event on the third lap, in its only Island appearance.

## RP

Born in 1916, Ronald Peck of Redbourne, Hertfordshire, was employed as a mechanical engineer draughtsman engaged in the design of large paper-converting machines, when in 1950 he decided to build his own four-cylinder 250 racer.

Given that his original childhoood interest was model-making, with the accent on tiny experimental internal combustion engines, the parallel of the model aircraft designer who managed to construct a full-size aircraft in the film *Flight of the Phoenix* will not be lost!

It was not until after the end of World War 2 that Peck actually became interested in motorcycles and the machine he chose to build was nothing less than a 250 cc double overhead-camshaft four-cylinder, unit-construction engine mounted in a rear-sprung racing motorcycle.

The fact that he lacked the facilities for such an ambitious task did not seem to daunt him. In his small 12 × 10 ft drawing office-cum-workshop he proceeded to design a 5-in. screw cutting lathe and a large bench-type vertical drill, then to manufacture the necessary wooden patterns and, subsequently, to machine and assemble the castings produced from those pattterns by a friend who owned a nearby factory.

Some 18 months later, with his precision-made equipment duly installed, he then set about the task of drawing in detail his dream powerplant, followed by a long bout of pattern-making and machining of castings and light alloy and steel billets to clearances more akin to those employed by watchmakers.

Bearing in mind the huge commitment of time involved with machining the vast number of special components, it is quite strange that Peck should have decided to use a bore and stroke of 44 × 41 mm for each of the tiny cylinders on the basis, 'because that would enable me to employ standard LE Velocette piston rings'. This added up to a capacity of 249 cc.

Created from a billet of Nitralloy steel, the one-piece disc type crankshaft was supported by no fewer than three plain and two roller bearings, the latter at the extremities of the shaft. Dural con-rods, machined from solid, ran direct on the crank and the gudgeon pins.

*Camshaft drive of the Roland Peck design*

The pistons were again from solid with steeply conical crowns with deep valve pockets and gave a compression ratio of 9 : 1.

Each cylinder barrel was a separate light-alloy assembly machined from scratch with a shrunk-in cast-iron liner. Light alloy was also used for the cylinder heads which had hemispherical combustion chambers with aluminium bronze valve seats.

Each camshaft was carried in three plain bearings—the centre one of the split variety. The cams operated direct, via shim adjusted thimbles, upon the valve stems, which were equipped with duplex springs. The camshaft drive was by a series of pinions and gears.

Lubrication was provided by a double gear type pump submerged in the 6-pint wet sump. The primary drive was by gear, and a truly superb piece of engineering. Between the crankshaft and gearbox was a short countershaft, carried on ball and roller bearings. Teeth cut on the rim of the crankshaft disc supported between the centre and timing-side plain bearings meshed with a pinion on the countershaft. The latter carried at its other end a pinion which in turn mated with a dished gear wheel bolted to

the clutch body and equipped with a shrouded vane-type rubber shock absorber.

A set of close-ratio gears of Burman manufacture were mounted in the main unit-construction casing, the standard Burman housing carrying the selector and kickstarter mechanism.

Having lavished so much time on the engine unit, Peck elected to use 'bought in' cycle parts, at least for the major components. The main frame was from a New Imperial with a Peck-designed and built swinging arm, and the forks—Webb girders, again modified by Peck, with light alloy links and double-friction damper plates.

The light alloy wheel hubs, equipped with Timken taper roller bearings, and the finned brake drums with shrunk in iron liners, were also home-made.

Peck built the RPS (Roland Peck Special) for his own personal enjoyment, rather than as a purely racing iron (hence the kickstarter and propstand). However, it did eventually get on to a race circuit but this was some five years later, in April 1958.

Since 1953 much had been done to the machine including a new frame built on Norton Featherbed lines with Earles type forks. Peck had also made new full-width brakes. There were also a number of other changes including a new 4-gallon alloy fuel tank and a small nose cone fairing at the front.

The machine was acquired by the well-known Leighton Buzzard dealer/tuner, Sid Mularney, early

*Brian Setchell with the RP four at Silverstone, April 1958, just prior to its first competitive outing*

in 1958, although its constructor still took an interest in its progress.

On 19 April 1958 the RPS was ridden by Brian Setchell at Silverstone. Before this the Amal carburettors had been bored out from $\frac{21}{32}$ in. to $\frac{23}{32}$ in., the inlet ports opened out to suit the slightly larger inlet valves fitted. Also, the lower compression rings were discarded. Maximum speed proved to be around 100 mph, but Setchell was handicapped by poor steering and rich carburation and finally one big-end tightened.

Over the next three years Mularney worked hard on the RPS. The problem he felt centred around the oiling system. And though there was plenty of oil pressure the engine persisted in breaking con-rods. After countless hours of testing and rebuilding Mularney constructed an oil pump that would provide twice the delivery of the original unit. By then maximum revs had risen from 9000 to 12,000 rpm and the compression ratio upped to 11.5:1. Another Mularney modification was to the front end where he first used BSA and later Manx Norton (shortened teledraulics. Finally, in an attempt to cure the less than satisfactory roadholding, a lightweight frame was constructed from Reynolds tubing.

But all this was to no real avail and Mularney eventually lost interest and the RPS passed to an Oxford enthusiast and then in 1965 to racer Mike Eglington who was a 23-year-old laboratory technician from Watford. Eglington spent three years restoring the machine before calling a halt due to lack of finance.

I wonder where this unique machine finally ended its days and if it still exists now? Perhaps someone out there knows. . . .

# 9
# Triumph Grand Prix

The history of the Triumph Grand Prix project can be traced directly to the machine used by Irishman Ernie Lyons to win the first post-war Senior Manx Grand Prix. His Triumph was also the first twin to win the famous event.

Held in dismally overcast conditions with rain and mist around various sections of the $37\frac{3}{4}$-mile Mountain Circuit, the 1946 Senior MGP was none the less watched by a vast gathering of spectators—many believed it to have been the largest in TT or MGP history up to that time.

The appalling weather conditions didn't seem to affect Lyons and he stormed away to win by 2 minutes 13 seconds, with an average speed of 76.74 mph from Ken Bills (Norton).

Although works bikes were not officially allowed in the Manx, Lyons' bike was in fact a factory 'special' expressly built for the event by the well-known tuner Freddie Clark, using Tiger 100 components and the light-alloy cylinder barrel and head from a wartime generator unit. It also employed one of Edward Turner's experimental sprung hubs.

But it was not until almost 18 months later that Triumph were to offer a replica of Lyons' victorious machine to the public which appeared as the Grand Prix model in January 1948.

Some might query why it took so long for Triumph to get around to actually making a move. For one thing the late 1940s was a period of intense production pressures, when it seemed that however many motorcycles were produced there were not enough to meet the demands of the transport hungry masses both at home and abroad. Triumph also took the opportunity to test their ideas further in the shape of the machine so successfully used by M. D. (David) Whitworth during 1947. Notable performances included the Belgian GP—where after leading on lap two he crashed, only to remount and finally finish fourth. Then in the Dutch TT the same rider gained a highly impressive rostrum position with a magnificent third. Added to these successes in the classics, Whitworth also won the *Circuit de la Cambre* in Belgium.

Another reason for the delay was that Freddie Clark had left Triumph to join AMC in January 1947 and that although based on the standard production 498 cc (63 × 80 mm) Tiger 100 and sharing these dimensions, the Grand Prix engine had a completely isolated set of components. Each GP was hand-built and specially tuned, and pumped out a claimed 40 bhp at 7200 rpm on pool petrol. Maximum speed was around the 120 mph mark and with empty tanks it weighed 310 lb. When one remembers the works

Right
*Ernie Lyons making the Triumph Grand Prix debut in the Ulster GP, August 1946. The following month, Lyons won the Senior Manx GP on the same bike*

Left
*David Whitworth receiving the winners' trophies after taking both the 350 and 500 races at the Grand Prix de Bruxelles, 22 June 1947. In the larger-capacity event, his mount was a Triumph Grand Prix*

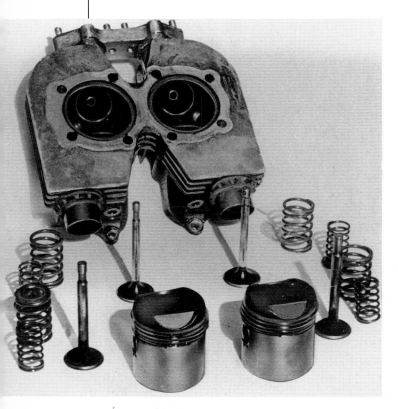

*Whitworth's 'factory' GP engine, 1947*

Right
*Whitworth in action during the 500 cc Belgian GP, 1947. He was leading on the second lap, but after a minor spill, finished fourth*

bikes raced by Lyons and Whitworth, Edward Turner's statement that 'it is not Triumph's policy to support racing with works machines and teams' seems rather naughty to say the least.

As already mentioned the cylinder and head were both in alloy, each barrel being fitted with a cast-iron liner. Unlike the later twin carburettor production Triumphs, the GP had parallel-mounted, rather than splayed instruments. Although the standard compression for the low octane pool petrol was only 8.3:1, higher compression pistons were also available more suitable for use with petrol benzole or methanol.

The more robust con-rods were special forgings in RR56 alloy and the plain big-ends were therefore able to function without liners. The lower halves of the big-ends were also made of RR56.

Built up and with the usual Triumph bolted-on central flywheel, the crankshaft *looked* standard. The crank members, however, were manufactured of case-hardened, nickel chrome steel of somewhat different section from that used in the Tiger 100.

This was specially hardened on the big-end journals and at the main bearings. These latter bearings comprised double-lipped rollers—distinct from the ball bearings used on the standard machine—and were chosen because of their greater load-carrying capacity.

The crankcase was almost standard, but had undergone slight variations in machining to make it suitable for the Grand Prix model.

A BTH racing magneto was fitted, together with manual ignition control.

Special camshafts provided a higher valve lift of longer duration, which had been developed in con-

junction with a tuned exhaust system featuring a separate exhaust pipe and megaphone assembly on each side of the machine.

Considerable efforts had been made to keep down the weight of reciprocating parts yet at the same time ensure their greatest possible strength. To this end duralumin pushrods were used, together with specially lightened and hardened tappets, with hard chrome faces. The tappet-guide block was made of RR56 alloy.

Lubrication was of the dry sump variety by means of large-bore plunger pumps and was therefore quite orthodox, but the oil tank held over a gal-

lon and had a special vent tower to take care of frothing at high rpm. A Vokes oil filter was adopted and fitted in the return side of the system.

Nickel chrome high-tensile gears were used in the gearbox, the ratios of which, with a 23-tooth engine sprocket, were 4.78, 5.24, 6.88 and 8.26 : 1. Alternative engine sprockets were available, giving a higher or lower set of close ratios.

As it was intended only for racing use no kick-starter was fitted. The clutch was a special, having extra spring pressure to accommodate the high engine torque. There were nine plates; five plain, four lined, the latter with special Ferodo inserts.

Above
*J. W. Raubi with his Triumph GP in the 1952
Hamilton 100 Senior Class, New Zealand*

Left
*A customer's Grand Prix engine, 1948. Note the
parallel-mounted carburettors and 'square' finning,
both hallmarks of the design*

The rev-counter was driven off the pinion that
on a standard model would have driven the dynamo
and the drive passed through holes in the front
engine plates.

The frame was of a brazed-up full cradle design
with forged lugs. The front forks, which followed
usual Triumph practice, were oil damped
teledraulics except that the springs were more suitable for racing use.

Both wheels had Dunlop alloy rims and the rear
Triumph sprung hub employed an 8 in. brake,
whilst the front was also an 8 in device. Tyre sizes
were 3.00 × 20 ribbed front and 3.50 × 19 studded
rear.

Finish was silver sheen and chrome, whilst the
1948 British price was £342 18s including purchase
tax (£72 18s).

No doubt remembering the performances of
Lyons and Whitworth, there were a fair number of
riders mounted on the new Triumph at the 1948 TT,
men such as Bob Foster, Freddie Frith and Ken Bills
together with several lesser known competitors. But
in the end only one Grand Prix lasted the distance—

*Triumph GP engine, showing remote float chamber, primary drive and magneto to advantage*

that of Norman Croft who finished 12th at 76.05 mph.

But at least Triumph's honour was partly restored when five Grand Prix machines finished in the first 12 in the year's Senior Manx GP, including the winner Don Crossley, who averaged 80.62 mph.

Whitworth again showed his form on the Continent by finishing fourth in the Dutch TT and fifth in Belgium. At the latter event Bob Foster finished fourth and Ken Bills sixth.

With the introduction of the World Championship Series in 1949, followed in 1950 by the availability of higher octane petrol, the success of the Triumph twin waned rapidly. So when the Triumph range for 1951 was announced at the end of 1950 the Grand Prix model had been deleted. In fact the company went as far as saying that the 1951 Tiger 100, modified with the aid of a £35 kit, could be made into a more potent machine than the pukka racing Grand Prix. . . . We can only speculate as to whether this was really true, or just a lame excuse for not wishing to develop its racing model any further.

# 10
# Two-strokes

As in Chapter 8 dealing with specials, it would be possible for this chapter on British two-strokes to fill a book, so once again I have selected ten types or *manufacturers*, although some of the concerns were little more than cottage industries. For the most part it covers the 1960s but of course there were British 'strokers' before this era, and there have certainly been some since. It was in the mid 1960s when marques such as Cotton, DMW and Greeves came to the fore with machinery capable of not only providing the clubman with an affordable racing iron, but also one capable of victory at British short circuits—even at the highest level.

Unfortunately, the era of the competitive British two-stroke racer was a short one, but even so it wasn't just the manufacturers who made their mark but a vast number of home-built models also appeared, including a four-cylinder 200 from Bert Fruin (1959), another 200, this time a disc valve single from Jim Bound (1960), the Blackburn built Anneley 125, the RCA 350 twin (late 1950s), Frank Highley's Merlin (1967) and the 125 Fahron (1968), to name but a few. There were also countless home-tuned BSA Bantams which were so popular that the Bantam Racing Club was formed in late 1960 to cater for their needs.

Finally, as with the four-strokes there were a

*Original DMW-framed, Alpha double-disc-valve twin, 1965*

*Alpha team, Snetterton, 1966: Mike Cutler, DMW Hornet/Alpha twin (29), Don Wolfindale, Royal Enfield GP5/Alpha twin (39), Fred Hadley, race mechanic (flat cap)*

number of significant 'white elephants' including the much publicized 250 Scorpion of 1964.

## Alpha Centuri

This Dudley-based specialist motorcycling engineering company can lay claim to being one of the very, very few British companies to survive the Japanese onslaught in the two-wheeled field, and today provide a full range of services aimed at the classic enthusiast.

Back in 1963 Alpha manufactured a host of engine components for nearly every motorcycle marque in Britain. To add to the ever-growing list of items as diverse as Excelsior crankshafts and Ariel big-end assemblies, Frank Cutler and his Alpha Automotive team designed and developed the bottom end of the Greeves RBS Silverstone racer. Unlike the other

manufacturers, such as not only Greeves, but also Cotton, DMW and Royal Enfield, Cutler could see by the summer of 1964 that the new Yamaha TD1 production racer would ultimately prove superior — once its poor reliability was overcome.

So Cutler decided to compete on equal terms by conceiving his own two-stroke twin. But not content with a Yamaha lookalike, he considered a whole range of alternatives. His answer was a 247 cc disc-induction vertical model. This was not as difficult a decision as you would expect. It was, quite simply, the best design solution. Cutler had problems though, for a start Alpha were then part of E. & H. P. Smith, who also owned Albion gearboxes. So Frank Cutler was forced to use an Albion HG5, together with all that gearbox's vices. This requirement also dictated the use of inboard discs, as they could be fitted anywhere other than on the ends of the crankshaft.

The Alpha 250 cc twin engine was gradually transformed into a three-dimensional object but without going into the expense of producing cylin-

*Don Wolfindale (left) and Dave Browning—Alpha team riders for 1967*

der and head patterns. Cutler thought he would look for proprietary items which could be suitably modified. This was an attempt to keep down development costs. He found that he could utilize cylinders from the Velocette Viceroy scooter (!) and the heads were from the BSA Bantam. It was in this form that the twin made its public debut in the 9 September 1965 issue of *The Motor Cycle*. This magazine published a couple of photographs showing a road-test machine and a stripped-down engine. The chassis was in fact an old DMW Hornet Mk1 racer which had been converted for road use and had in its time housed a number of other projects including the infamous peripheral-valve 250 single. Cutler's son, Mike, remembers that out of all the machines he rode this was the one which 'provided the most fun'. When explained in more detail 'fun' transpired to

be heart-stopping moments introduced by evil handling!

Even though the prototype engine was mounted in a chassis which didn't handle, the motor proved a resounding success. So, with 1000 or so miles on the clock, patterns for racing barrels and heads were commissioned. With (the unpaid) Fred Hadley assisting with the project, Frank Cutler and his son completed the machining and final development out of hours, so the completed Alpha twin, now christened Centuri, hadn't cost the company half as much as they had expected.

Frank Cutler's basic design consisted of a 247 cc, 180-degree twin, but with a square bore and stroke, of 54 × 54 mm which, due entirely to the gearbox, was fitted with twin, centrally-mounted inboard discs. These 0.020 in. thick spring steel discs, one per cylinder, were mounted on hexagonal carriers which, in turn, were keyed to the crankshaft centre. Acting in the normal disc-valve fashion, the asymmetrical inlet timing could be varied to obtain the required engine characteristics. But due to their central location, only one inlet tract could be fitted. A 29 mm Dell'Orto SS1 carburettor was finally chosen and a huge 1600, yes *1600*, main jet was fitted. This ensured that the engine always received more than its share of the 20 : 1 petrol/oil mixture. Mike Cutler recalls removing the main jet altogether and the engine running perfectly without it! When an Alpha Centuri engine was first tried by DMW they didn't believe the 1600 jet, and fitted a 400 in its place, promptly suffering a piston seizure within 200 yards.

The rest of the crankshaft was just as unorthodox as the induction gear, with four out of its five main bearings running directly on the shafts themselves. The assembly, which was finally fitted into the Centuri vertically-split crankcases, contained a large centrally-mounted alloy casting housing two roller bearings, one ball roller bearing and a pair of oil seals. But just to complicate matters it also carried the inner and outer disc housings. The duplex chain primary drive was taken from the nearside crank end, while the other end drove a pair of Mini Cooper contact breakers and the rev-counter.

While on the subject of primary drive, Frank Cutler cured the problems associated with the ultra-heavy Albion clutch by manufacturing an all new unit, with an alloy drum and bronze/steel plates. In fact, the bronze plates were turned down from 12 in. Caterpillar bulldozer parts! Although still running in an oil bath, the new clutch ran without problems and proved a 100 per cent improvement over the six-spring Albion unit it replaced. The Albion HG5 gearbox which the team had to use was well known for its weak, indifferent gear selection, but its biggest fault was a trait which attempted to select two gears at once. This little idiosyncrasy was so bad that it even prompted Greeves (who used the same gearbox on their 1965 RBS Silverstone) to supply a four-speed conversion and as soon as Albion came up with their new barrel-cam, five-speed box, Frank Cutler dropped the HG5 like a hot brick.

The sand-cast alloy barrels were fitted with 0.185 in. thick spun cast-iron liners, which contained some very interesting, and again unconventional, porting. As well as the main transfer ports, Cutler had positioned a pair of auxiliary ports between them and the single oval exhaust port.

Amazingly Cutler's idea was a full five years ahead of Yamaha's similar design for their quick TD2 racers which first appeared in 1969. Radial-finned 12 : 1 heads were held down to the barrels by four through-studs and centrally located, long-reach 14 mm spark plugs protruded into a conventional 'top hat', squish-shaped combustion chamber.

Royal Enfield, then also part of the E. & H. P. Smith group, grudgingly supplied the Alpha team a GP5 rolling chassis, but with the proviso that it had to remain standard. These restrictions were due to Enfield's only being allowed to develop a single-cylinder racer, and prevented Alpha from placing the engine where they thought best in the frame. The result of this silly rule was that the Centuri twin had to be mounted too far back in the frame, thus enabling the twin expansion chambers to clear the Enfield's duplex front downtubes. Mike Cutler describes the handling as poor and not to be compared with the original DMW-framed Centuri on which 'works' rider Don Wolfindale scored three straight wins from three starts. (The other official Alpha pilot was Dave Browning.) The Enfield running gear was fortunately short-lived as Enfield's Redditch factory closed its race shop a few months later. So from then onwards Alpha could use whatever engine location, or for that matter chassis, they wished.

As Enfield withdrew from the scene, Frank Cutler was able to snap up their now redundant Heenan & Froude DPXO dyno. This enabled him to improve the Centuri engine and also to confirm the power output, which he'd been unable to do at the Alpha factory in Dudley because of noise restrictions. The brake was installed at another local firm, Graham Starr

*Alpha 247 cc Centuri engine with single Dell'Orto SS1 carburettor*

Engineering, and it was from this test shop that most of the future development work was undertaken.

In its most powerful form the Centuri twin was claimed to develop 47 bhp at 12,200 rpm. With this kind of power the Alpha engine should have been the natural successor to the Greeves Silverstone and various Villiers Starmaker-powered racers, for a new generation of British raceware. Sadly, this was not to be. In reality the only paying customers were DMW, who took a couple of units, and leading Cadwell Park specialist John Kirkby.

At the beginning of 1968, Kirkby and his brother Ray (his race mechanic) purchased the only 'private' Centuri engine from Alpha. The engine was mounted in Kirkby's ex-Tom Philips, Vic Camp Ducati Mach 1. After solving the problem of installing the Alpha in the Ducati chassis, the newcomer made its race debut at a Cadwell club meeting in March 1968. Kirkby was rewarded when the Alpha/Ducati screamed home to record two wins, beating Bob Heath on a DMW in the first race even though no rev-counter was fitted and the bike was hopelessly over-geared.

These victories were followed by numerous wins and top places throughout the season against stars such as Derek Chatterton, Stan Woods and Steve Machin. Sadly, this early promise could not be further developed as later in 1968 E. & H. P. Smith pulled the plug on any further racing and not only was Kirkby denied spares (Alpha repurchased his engine), but to quote Mike Cutler, 'No further Centuri engines or spares were to be sold'. Thus read the directive from the Smith group management.

This was a disaster. All the work put into the project was wasted. There had been eight Centuri engines completed, with a further 25 to be built from components already manufactured. Just why the short-sighted decision was taken remains a mystery, but with it went the final British hope of keeping abreast of the rapidly improving Japanese hardware.

Today, Mike Cutler has ensured that a piece of British racing history can at least be seen by today's fans, with regular appearances on a Centuri in Classic Racing Motorcycle Club parades around the country. You are left wondering just what this exciting machine might have achieved had it been allowed to. . . .

*Hermann Meier with the Michael O'Rourke Arrow, Silverstone, March 1960*

Meanwhile, Fred Hadley had become involved in the 125 Starr-Hadley project. Built in 1968, this was virtually half an Alpha Centuri engine with a Royal Enfield gearbox. But like its bigger cousin this too was destined to run foul of the Smith group's 'no racing' policy.

## Ariel Arrow

Prior to 1958 the Ariel factory had been well known for its traditional British four-stroke big singles and twins and they had even tried their hands with a 200 single, the Colt. Two-strokes?...never, but all this was set to change as in July of that year the Leader was launched.

This was a 54 × 54 mm parallel twin piston ported two-stroke with a capacity of 247 cc. The Leader had been designed by Val Page and was perhaps the most unorthodox small capacity motorcycle to reach production in Britain during the late 1950s.

To a conservative industry the new Ariel was a major step forward, not only because of its twin-cylinder two-stroke engine, but the full enclosure—

Above
*O'Rourke finished a brilliant seventh in the 1960 Lightweight TT*

*The Meier-tuned engine assembly*

built-in legshields and screen, pressed-steel frame and many other unique features.

The cylinders were inclined forward at 45 degrees with the firing interval at 180 degrees. The engine porting was conventional for the time with the inlet at the rear of the cylinder, exhaust at the front, transfers to each side of each bore and all timings piston controlled. On the roadster there was only one carburettor, which was to prove a nuisance to the many Ariel tuners who were to appear later.

The engine and gearbox were assembled into a single light alloy casting and this was to form the two crankcases for the engine with a central dividing wall. The front of these cases was liberally finned for cooling. Gearbox was a four-speeder and primary drive was by simplex chain. The original barrels were cast iron, with alloy heads.

The success of the Leader soon led to the Arrow series which began in late 1960, the Super Sport (often known as the Golden Arrow) in 1961 and finally in 1964 a 199.5 cc underbored version. But the baby Arrow's life was to be short, as all Ariel production (including the two-strokes) was halted in late 1965.

Officially the Selly Oak factory didn't make any racers. But various factory personnel started to develop the standard engine to racing specification. This continued well into the 1960s and the changes included twin carburettor crankcases, alloy cylinders, special cast heads, close-ratio gear clusters and even a batch of racing crankshafts made by the Alpha company.

Most of this 'illegal' factory race development was carried out by an impressive list of individuals including Peter Inchley, Hermann Meier, Sammy Miller, Roger Barlow and even Val Page. By this time Ariel was owned by the BSA Group, and heaven knows what its corporate bosses would have done if they had found out.

But this clandestine activity was to benefit several riders including not only Peter Inchley himself, but Robin Good, George Salt, Michael O'Rourke and Cecil Sandford.

The very first to appear was the O'Rourke machine which, entered by Harold Daniell and tuned by Hermann Meier, made its bow at the Hutchinson 100 meeting in early April 1960. In the event, after being a highly impressive fourth fastest 250 in practice, O'Rourke lay tenth in the race until a piston tightened on the fourth lap.

*Thruxton 500-miler, 25 June 1960. Cecil Sandford is seen on the second-place machine*

*The Earles Arrow four on the test-bed at the Ariel factory. Note sandcast heads*

If this was a disappointment what followed certainly wasn't. First at Brands Hatch in mid May, O'Rourke took the Meier tuned Arrow past Shorey and Hardy on NSUs and then Hailwood's twin-cylinder desmo Ducati to lead the 250 cc race. Even

*MGP (Michael and Gerald Piper) four-cylinder Arrow racer, 1968*

though he was eventually forced back to fourth O'Rourke had opened more than a few eyes. Then came the TT in June, where the Ariel twin created a sensation when O'Rourke proved its speed *and* reliability by not only being the best placed British machine, but finishing seventh at an average speed of 80.18 mph—only 30 seconds behind sixth place-man Taniguichi on a works Honda four—and in front of some glamorous foreign machinery including MV Agusta, Bianchi and NSU.

The reliability of the Ariel under racing conditions was emphasized later that month when Cecil Sandford and Sammy Miller came home second in the 250 cc class of the Thruxton 500-mile endurance race. Another Selly Oak twin finished third. In fact if Miller hadn't stepped off in the early stages and damaged the machine, it would probably have won comfortably.

A year later Robin Good and Peter Inchley again came second, with another Ariel fourth. But Sandford and Miller were forced out after 65 laps with engine seizure.

In 1962 victory once more eluded the Selly Oak men when Good and Inchley once again finished second, with Sandford and 'new' co-rider O'Rourke third.

But somehow Ariel missed a golden opportunity to cash in on the over-the-counter racing boom and it was left to the likes of their smaller rivals, like Greeves and Cotton, to make the running. One can only speculate at what might have been.

The Ariel engine was also used in a number of

interesting specials, notably the Ernie Earles-built 498 cc Arrow sidecar outfit. Raced by Bill Boddice this used two Arrow engines alongside each other, but although it was fast it was hopelessly unreliable. The Earles Arrow four first appeared in 1960 and was used until the end of 1962.

Another 'four' was the later machine built by brothers Gerald and Michael Piper. Unlike the Earles machine this was a solo and the engines were mounted one above the other in a similar fashion to the Yamaha 250 four of the late 1960s. Cycle parts were largely Norton.

Other home-built Arrow projects were a three-cylinder raced by Harry Price and even half-an-Arrow—a single-cylinder 125 which made its debut at a Silverstone practice day in early 1960.

Arrow engines were also successfully used in sprinting with many a ftd (fastest time of the day) in the 250 cc category being set by one of the Ariel 'strokers' during the 1960s.

Today various converted Leaders or Arrows are quite often to be seen at either Vintage or Classic events. In many ways they are an ideal machine, being simple, cheap and easy to tune.

Above
*Harry Price on the Schwindt Ariel 3, Mallory Park, 29 October 1967*

Below
*A 124 cc, single-cylinder, 'half-an-Arrow' racer, Silverstone practice day, 7 March 1960*

## Cotton Telstar

Winners of the 1923 Junior TT and 1926 Light-weight race, the Gloucester Cotton concern stormed back into the racing spotlight when short-circuit star, Derek Minter, won the 1964 ACU 250 cc Star—the equivalent of the British Championship on a 247 cc (68 × 68 mm) Cotton Telstar.

The Telstar was the first of Britain's new generation 'formula junior' specification racers to be publicly announced in October 1962. The machine had been sparked off by the introduction of the Villiers Starmaker engine, *and* like the Greeves Silverstone, by the efforts of a private rider. In Cotton's case, this was Peter Vallis, who had campaigned a racerized scrambler with some success during the 1962 season.

*Derek Minter, Cotton's factory rider, Snetterton, April 1965. This machine had a specially tuned engine and a six-speed box*

Although the Villiers company had their own dynamometer, it was Cotton who primarily race-developed the new Starmaker engine. This started as early as October 1962 and the Cotton staff included Fluff Brown—who now runs the FB-AJS concern at Andover.

Minter was signed up in time for the 1963 season and responded by finishing an impressive second—behind Ducati desmo twin-mounted Mike Hailwood—at the Mallory Park season opener in March that year. But most of 1963 was spent squeezing out not only more power but reliability too. These early engines were what one might truthfully describe as fragile.

Minter's works bike received a variety of modifications such as remote contact breakers, single Amal GP carburettor and a more rigid cylinder liner.

However, the most important of these changes came in June 1964 in the form of a six-speed gearbox, which was needed to overcome the narrowing

*The Frank Higley-sponsored Cotton at Thruxton, 1 August 1965. Rider Bill Ivy won the 250 cc race*

powerband of Minter's rapidly developing factory engine. The only other Cotton with this gearbox was the equally rapid Frank Higley-sponsored machine ridden by the talented Bill Ivy.

Minter's (and Ivy's) engines progressed from the original 25 bhp at 6500 rpm to 31.2 bhp at 7800 rpm. This was more or less the power available when Derek Minter rode his Telstar to victory in the 1964 250 ACU Star championship. However, it wasn't the engine alone that took the title—it was the skill of a superb rider combined with the good handling characteristics of the 230 lb lightweight machine that claimed this well-earned and well-deserved success.

Cotton had, at that time, been manufacturing motorcycles for the past 40 years or so and obviously knew a thing or two when it came to making them handle. Their frame consisted of a full duplex layout, manufactured from seamless 'A' grade cold drawn steel tubing. The top rail and swinging arm were

*Standard 1965 Cotton Telstar with four speeds*

constructed of $1\frac{1}{8}$ in. × 14 swg with the cradle and subframe made from $\frac{7}{8}$ in. × 14 swg.

The fact of the matter was that Cotton manufactured little else apart from the frame and the swinging arm, for they employed Armstrong leading-link front forks and rear units (later models used Girling items) to control the machine's suspension.

The first models were fitted with the infamous

6 in. SLS British Hub Company's CD brake assemblies both back and front. However, the 6 in. front brake, famous for its lack of effect, was soon changed and by 1964 the Telstar, along with the Greeves Silverstone, sported the newly-introduced $7\frac{1}{2}$ in. TLS unit, which British Hub had produced to quell the many complaints arising from the original 6 in. front stopper.

Unlike machines from other factories such as DMW, Greeves and Enfield, the Telstar was fitted with 19 in. wheels front and rear throughout its whole production period. This, if one considers modern trends, should have been to their disadvantage, however, it does not seem to have hampered the style of works rider Derek Minter who, along with Frank Higley's rider Bill Ivy, claimed victory after victory aboard these two-stroke flyers.

When tested by *Motor Cycling* in their 21 November 1964 issue, works rider Minter and *Motor Cycling* staffman Bruce Main-Smith rode one of the latest four-speed production models. Held over the 1.6-mile Silverstone Club circuit, the best flying lap put

**Above**
*Brands 500-miler, 26 June 1966. Reg Everett is seen on the class-winning Cotton Conquest*

**Left**
*Snetterton, 29 May 1966 — last lap of the 250 cc race at Riches Corner. Reg Everett (Yamaha, 18) lost control, while Derek Minter (Cotton, 11) went on to win the event. Peter Inchley (Villiers special, 16) also crashed a few moments later*

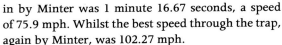

oured fibreglass ware styled in the classic British racer fashion.

The majority of Telstar production occurred during 1964–5 and by the time of its demise in 1967 over 60 machines had been produced. They have found their way to various corners of the globe with Australia at present holding the honour of the highest numbered example — machine number 66.

Once Minter left at the end of 1966, Cotton's fortunes soon deteriorated rapidly, as by then the Yamaha twin was beginning its surge to the top as *the* clubman's mount and in the process making all the singles obsolete almost overnight.

The only area where the Cotton could still compete after this was in the production class. They achieved a high level of success with the Conquest which was essentially a Telstar with lights at even the highest level. There were class victories at venues throughout Britain with riders such as Minter, Inchley and Everett. The highlights without doubt were class wins at the prestigious 500-mile races at Castle Coombe in 1965 by Minter/Inchley (they also finished third overall) and Inchley/Everett at Brands Hatch the following year.

The 1966 Brands Hatch 500-miler class winner

in by Minter was 1 minute 16.67 seconds, a speed of 75.9 mph. Whilst the best speed through the trap, again by Minter, was 102.27 mph.

A distinctive feature of the Telstar was its Mitchenhall (Avon) fibreglass ware. On introduction the Telstar was equipped with a 2½-gallon jelly mould continental style fuel tank and a rather awkward looking single-piece fairing. However, with the Mk 2's appearance in 1964 the fuel tank, seat and fairing came in for a change and the Telstar now looked far more conventional with its maroon col-

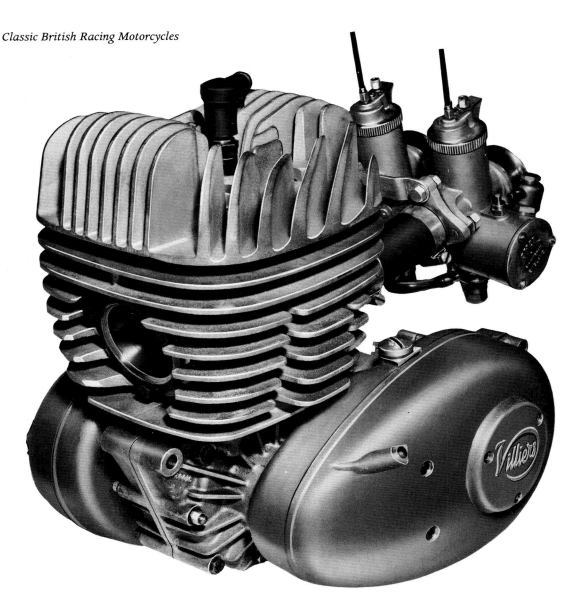

*The 1963 version of the Villiers Starmaker racing engine used by DMW and others, and featuring twin Amal Monobloc carburettors*

had the full treatment: racer head and barrel, close ratio gears, external contact breaker assembly, alloy rims, racing tyres, large fibreglass tank, racing seat, clip-ons, rear-sets, rev-counter, direct lighting and air scoop for the front brake.

Manx GP winner Paddy Reid was still cleaning up with his Conquest into the early 1970s—even in the open class at Cadwell Park Club events. A total of 166 Conquests were produced and the price (in 1966) was between £279 and £350 depending on exact specification.

Today it is quite often possible to see both the Telstar and Conquest in action at classic racing events.

## DMW Hornet & Typhoon

The first DMW (Dudley Motor Works) Hornet was launched at the Earls Court Show back in November 1953 and it was not a two-stroke, but an extremely neat little bike powered by a French AMC (Ateliers de Mecanique du Centre) 125 cc dohc engine. But although still listed (at a whopping £362 10s) a year later it was unlikely that any other than the proto-type was ever actually constructed.

It was not to be until several years later that the name was to be given to another of the Dudley, Worcestershire company's products.

In October 1962 the Villiers company announced their all new 247 cc Starmaker engine. As with rivals Cotton, DMW were quick to follow this up with the launch of a Starmaker-powered road racer. Housed in a modified DMW competitions frame—which employed a large diameter top tube, tapered front down member and light-alloy engine plates—this first prototype also had Metal Profiles spring-controlled forks with an independent damper unit mounted between the fork legs in front of the steering head. Other details included full width brake hubs, round section swinging arm and a twin carburettor Starmaker motocross engine.

For 1963 the factory carried out a considerable amount of development work including a new duplex chassis (but still with round swinging arm) and a single $1\frac{3}{8}$ in. Amal Monobloc carburettor which was soon replaced by a $1\frac{1}{2}$ in. 3GP2 from the same source. Riders that year included Australian Jack Findlay and British short-circuit specialist John Dixon, with Findlay proving that the DMW was competitive by working up to sixth spot in the Lightweight TT before crashing on the fifth lap.

There were no production Hornets in 1963, but bowing to the ever-increasing demands of DMW and

others in 1964 Villiers produced a close finned road racing engine, fittted with outrigger contact breakers, close ratio gearbox and an Amal 3GP2 carburettor. Code-named the 834E the engine boasted a full circle crankshaft, energy transfer magneto and was far more suited to the rigours of short-circuit racing than a tuned scrambles motor. The production version of the Hornet known as the Mk 1 came complete with a $3\frac{1}{2}$-gallon alloy petrol tank and a Bill Jakeman fairing but had interestingly gained a few pounds in the transference from its prototype form. However, this didn't stop the enthusiastic clubmen who were looking for something different and cheaper than the quick but expensive 250 Bultaco and Aermacchis.

As time progressed DMW, headed by the enthusiastic Harold Nock, found itself looking for an alter-

*Aussie Jack Findlay with the works DMW Hornet, Lightweight TT, 10 June 1963*

*Classic British Racing Motorcycles*

*Hornets at Darley Moor races, 2 April 1966 — P. Humber (36) and R. J. Minster (35)*

*Hornet Mark 2 in factory-fresh finish*

native power unit, but in the mid 1960s only Greeves and Royal Enfield were producing machines with suitable engines. However, at the heart of both of these lay the Frank Cutler-designed Alpha crankshaft assembly and in the case of the Enfield GP5 the complete bottom end was Alpha.

Nock lost no time in recruiting the services of Alpha Bearings and within a short time they had produced a 68 mm stroke racing crankshaft/crankcase assembly which just happened to be compatible with a Villiers Starmaker cylinder. However, the main difference was that this new bottom end had been designed to accommodate the Albion five-speed barrel cam gearbox, which was needed to cope with the higher output and narrower powerband supplied by the 68 mm bore of the Peter Inchley-designed cylinders. This motor, fitted with an Albion racing clutch and DMW chain cases, formed the power unit of the Hornet Mk 2 (2HO), which on introduction in 1966 sold for the sum of £425. The new Mk 2 utilized the Mk 1 frame and forks but now listed an Italian Oldani TLS front brake as an option.

One item that all the Hornets had in common was the unique MP (Metal Profile) front forks. As can be seen from the illustrations the complete assembly was way ahead of its time and boasted instant spring preloaded adjustments offered by the centrally mounted single Girling suspension unit. The mounting bracket for this unit also acted as a top slider brace which, within the last few years, has become standard practice among the racing fraternity.

All DMW Hornet frames were similar and had a single 1¾ in. diameter 14 swg top rail and 1 in. diameter 15 swg cradle loops, which produced a taut and light steering machine that handled superbly. The Mk 1 and 2 were joined in 1967 by the last of the Hornets—the new 250 'Twin'.

This machine employed the same tubular steel 52 in. wheelbase Hornet frame but was fitted with the incredibly rapid Alpha Centuri rotary disc induction twin. The 12,000 rpm engine was unusual in that it employed only one rotary disc, which was centrally mounted and fed by a lone 27 mm Dell'Orto SS1 carburettor.

The development of the 54 × 54 mm racing engine conjures up pictures of endless hours sweating over a hot dynamometer. However, nothing could be further from the truth as this motor covered over 1000 miles of everyday running in a DMW roadster machine. The test ended with extremely satisfactory results and nothing had failed or seized during its brief but arduous excursions on the public highway.

*First EMC racer, the 250 split single. One of these had considerable success in the hands of Les Archer, including victory in the 1947 Hutchinson 100*

*Harold Nock-inspired 500 Typhoon, circa 1965—essentially a pair of Starmaker engines. This interesting project never entered production*

Again the Alpha-constructed Centuri engine was capable of being fitted with an Albion five-speed gearbox which was easily accommodated by the Hornet frame. However, the new engine was more powerful than the 35 bhp Alpha-based single. In its final but fragile form it developed 47 bhp, however, due to marginal reliability this was reduced to 44 bhp. Only two AHO twins were actually built and these were offered for sale in 1967–8 for £495.

Probably the most famous victory by a Hornet was by the six-speed works bike which Bill Smith used to win the 1964 Southern 100. In many ways this was the DMW equivalent of the special Cottons raced by Minter and Ivy.

Besides its 250, DMW also came up with the Harold Nock-inspired Typhoon in 1965. This was essentially a double up of the 68 × 68 mm Starmaker top end with purpose-built crankcases, giving an overall capacity of 494 cc. There were also alternative flywheels and shaft assemblies which used the 66 × 72 mm bore and stroke, so that experiments could be carried out using Villiers 36A and Royal Enfield GP5 type barrels.

Crankcases and shaft assemblies were built in co-operation with Alpha. Each engine shaft had two main bearings, giving the double engine a four bearing shaft. The outer ends were closed so that only one seal per shaft was necessary. Air space between the barrels and especially around the inner main bearings was generous yet overall width at shaft level was only 14½ in.—compared to the 15 in. overall of the conventional Starmaker.

From coupled shafts the drive was taken by

**Above**
*EMC-Puch 125 customer's racer, available 1951–3. It made more noise than speed*

**Right**
*Streamlined EMC-Puch at 1954 TT*

pinions to a countershaft supported in a specially wide, double-row Alpha roller bearing. A pinion on the nearside (left) of the countershaft meshed with the clutch of the Albion five-speed box.

Clutch components were substantially those of the Royal Enfield 736 cc Interceptor with full friction surfaces.

A take-off pinion above the transmission train drove, on the nearside, the rev-counter gearbox and on the offside, the enclosed twin contact breaker assembly. An advantage of this arrangement was that the points were isolated from possible vibration and undisturbed when either engine was detached. Ignition was by battery and twin coils and with an eye to possible future development of a roadster version the crankcase design was such that either of the outer bosses could be machined to accommodate a

Above
*Mike Hailwood on the EMC 125, West German GP, 1962. He finished third at an average speed of 83.39 mph, a magnificent achievement against a horde of Japanese works bikes*

Above left
*F. H. Burman's 250 EMC-Puch, 1955*

Left
*Dr Ehrlich (second left) with his team of helpers at the De Havilland Engine Company, 1960. Rider Rex Avery is seated on the latest 125 EMC single*

Lucas alternator. The frame followed Hornet lines, but with the tubing sizes increased from 1 in. to 1⅛ in. diameter.

The only non British component on this 60 bhp machine was the Italian Fontana four leading-shoe front brake.

Sadly no production versions were built.

## EMC

To trace the origin of EMC one must go back to 1937 when Dr Josef Ehrlich, then in his twenties, arrived from Austria seeking to further his career in the field of two-stroke engineering. Two years later saw the

first of his engines but it took a further seven years of research to come up with a machine that would be a viable proposition in quantity production and attract the city money that was needed to start the ball rolling. With the necessary backing acquired, Dr Ehrlich went into production in 1947 with his 350 split-single two-stroke, which at the time was priced at a very competitive £157. Operating from a factory in Park Royal, north-west London, EMC Ltd, (Ehrlich Motor Company) produced a modest 10 to 12 machines per week. But the 350 cc aircooled machine, equipped with a rigid back end failed to stir the imagination of the then conservative British motorcycling public.

Development continued and a plunger rear suspension was soon produced. This added up to quite an impressive specification which included telescopic forks, Burman four-speed gearbox, auto oiling system and duplex frame. The handling and performance at the time were reported by *The Motor Cycle* to be of a very high order but even this did little to improve sales of the 80 mph roadster.

It wasn't that the new EMC failed to live up to any of its many claimed abilities—it just looked different. The large, square sparsely finned alloy cylinder not unlike the Greeves Silverstone/

*Experimental 250 cc EMC racing engine, 1962*

Challenger of the mid 1960s, was fitted with two high-level rear facing exhaust systems and the oddly mounted carburettor didn't help much either. The British public wanted a machine that looked like a motorcycle and the EMC didn't fit the bill—it was too radical. So, unfortunately, due to lack of sales, production was brought to a close in late 1952, after only 1200 machines had rolled out of the factory doors. The company folded in March 1953.

However, the factory hadn't been without its competition successes. Les Archer, riding a 250 cc DKW-based EMC, claimed the Mellano Trophy at the 1947 Hutchinson 100. But the racing EMCs didn't have much in common with their production counterparts. They were still split singles but were watercooled and equipped with a third forward facing piston, which acted as a compressor/supercharger, and bore a striking resemblance to the illustrious 250/350 pre-war DKWs.

The first of a long line of racing 125 cc EMCs were introduced in 1952. But this time the factory employed an Austrian Puch engine, again a split single but aircooled, and of course unblown.

A past owner/rider of one of these machines des-cribed it as having a top speed of around 75 mph which sounded like 175 mph. The short open mega-phone exhaust system of this ultra-lightweight was responsible for this incredible din and it has been said that in the 1952 TT, F. Burman, who finished in sixth place, could be heard approaching from a distance of over five miles!

It is a little remembered fact that John Surtees was entered by Dr Ehrlich in the 1953 Ultra Light-weight TT on a 125 EMC-Puch. However, this was not to be a happy occasion, particularly for Surtees as he spilled near Ballaugh during practice, due to mechanical failure, sustaining hand injuries which were subsequently to put him out of action for the entire programme. This was of particular annoyance, as Surtees recalled recently in a television pro-gramme, as he had been offered a works Norton ride for the first time.

Disillusioned by the rigours of motorcycle manufacturing (and quite likely the flak he received regarding the Surtees incident) Dr Ehrlich then joined the Austin car company to assist with new vehicle development. Whilst there he designed a twin split-single two-stroke engine for the then revolutionary Austin Mini. Unfortunately the four-piston two-stroke unit was a shade too revolutionary for the Austin board and so the project never passed beyond the prototype stage.

During this period (the late 1950s), the aircraft industry, due to substantial fall-off of both military and civilian sales, were looking to diversify their vast, but now largely dormant, production capacity. And so like many others the De Havilland aircraft company decided that the production of industrial engines was the way to solve many of their problems. They set to and produced a small 150 cc two-stroke unit which could only be described as a total and absolute disaster.

Hearing about their plight Dr Ehrlich approached De Havilland and in 1958 offered to assist. With sensible porting Dr Ehrlich achieved results that De Havilland had previously thought to be unobtainable. But this 150 cc loop scavenge two-stroke was no more advanced than the engine that he'd been toying with while at Austins. In fact, it was during the 1950s that he had patented a number of ideas which formed the nucleus of his future developments.

Prior to joining De Havilland, Dr Ehrlich had been involved in a horrific car accident, the injuries sustained from it plaguing him for a number of years, but they didn't stop him working. Operating out of De Havilland at Leavesden, north Watford, and now

the small engine division chief, Dr Ehrlich proceeded to develop a number of small two-stroke engines. Based on a single-cylinder of the racing DKW three-cylinder he adapted the design to suit a whole range of prototype vehicles, which included a 150 cc 80 mph road bike, a 150 cc scooter, a 150 cc outboard motor and even a two-stroke dumper-truck.

The primary aim was to rival Villiers in commercial and motorcycle engine sales. However, to succeed an awful lot of development was necessary if he was to build stronger and more powerful engines than Villiers.

Early in 1959 the factory were up to their ears in piston ported engines but suddenly later that year the team produced a rotary disc induction 125, which was very similar to the East German MZ developed by Walter Kaaden. However, the water-cooled single was fitted with a finned cylinder, as opposed to the bald MZ version, which was produced at a local foundry, Browns of Hitchin.

In 1960 Dr Ehrlich employed this engine in one of the antiquated Puch frames that were last seen

*A machine which promised so much and delivered so little, the 1964 125 cc EMC twin. This watercooled design was intended to take a full crack at World Championship honours. Unfortunately, it proved pitifully slow*

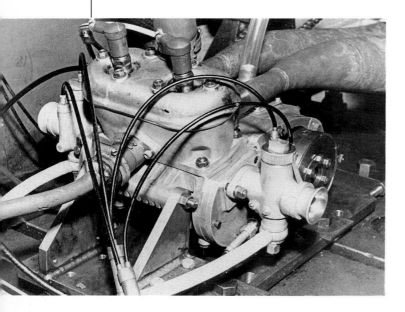

*Disc-valve, watercooled, 125 cc EMC twin engine on test-bed, August 1963*

*O. B. 'Bert' Greeves and one of the first production RAS Silverstones, March 1963*

in the mid 1950s but despite the indifferent handling early tests proved very successful. All that was required was the services of a good rider. Dr Ehrlich came up trumps and found his man working as a toolmaker not 200 yards away in the main De Havilland factory. Rex Avery, an established Norton rider, was only too happy to transfer to the small engine division and become the unofficial factory rider.

The 54 × 54 mm six-speed engine was light years ahead of its competition and the original 23½ bhp engine fitted with barrel 'C' (works coding) proved unbeatable throughout the 1960 season. Rex was establishing lap records left, right and centre but as time went by lap times dropped and successes became fewer.

The original engine, while only producing 23½ bhp at 10,000 rpm, had a powerband of 2000 rpm but later developed engines, although giving 27 bhp, had powerbands of only 800 rpm making them extremely difficult to ride. Another problem with the machine was vibration. Rex was used to this and had calloused hands to prove it.

Recognizing that the days of the 125 singles were numbered Dr Ehrlich set to and scaled down its com-

ponents to form an all new 43 × 43 mm 125 twin. The first run on the dynamometer showed a disappointing 16 bhp but with much work this finally came up to approximately 25 bhp.

Rex hoped the twin, with its impressive chassis, would put him back on top but the new machine was only practised a couple of times and raced once before being retired to a dark corner of the Leavesden factory. Its powerband was an incredibly narrow 300 rpm, which prevented the engine pulling from one gear to the next. The final blow came at its Brands debut when it was passed down the straight by a home-tuned BSA Bantam. Rather than continue Rex pulled out and so ended its first and only race.

This ended a period in history which reads like the who's who of racers. Mike Hailwood, Derek Minter, Paddy Driver, Rex Avery, Tony Godfrey, Peter Williams and many more, all rode the EMC with varying degrees of success. However, the high point of this era has to be when Dr Ehrlich's team finished a magnificent third, fourth and fifth in the 1962 Belgian GP (Driver, Hailwood and Avery), with Hailwood taking third spot the following week in the West German GP. However, from this point Japanese technology dropped into overdrive and sped away from the little Hertfordshire factory with designs such as the five-cylinder Honda 125, the Suzuki 125 twin and the 41 bhp Yamaha V4.

During his stay at Leavesden Dr Ehrlich had produced, on a consultancy basis, designs for other factories. But it was the ill-fated Manx lottery, supposedly financing the next British world beater, that prompted his most ambitious design, a 500 cc water-cooled rotary disc induction square four two-stroke. The drawing still exists today to prove its paper existence.

In 1965 the De Havilland group of companies was taken over by the aero engine giants Rolls-Royce. This left Dr Ehrlich and his team high and dry as one of the first things Rolls-Royce did was to dissolve the small engine division, which meant that Dr Ehrlich now had to finance his own two-stroke research or retire.

He chose to set up on his own in a small factory unit in Bletchley, Buckinghamshire. From there he carried out a number of development contracts, including racing outboard engines—and even an engine for a lawn mower! Then came a period in the 1970s when Dr Ehrlich turned his attention to Formula 3 car racing, before returning once more in the next decade to his original love, motorcycles.

After a short-lived association with the ill-fated

*Reg Everett, the man whose performances on a homebuilt special during 1962 convinced Bert Greeves to market a racer for the following season*

Overleaf
*Dave Simmonds with his 1964 RBS Silverstone at Brands Hatch that year*

Waddon enterprise, Dr Ehrlich was to taste perhaps his biggest moment of glory ever when Andy Watts took his EMC-Rotax-powered machine to a brilliant second spot in the 1984 250 cc British GP at Silverstone.

## Greeves Silverstone and Oulton

Oscar Bertrum (Bert) Greeves was very much a lone wolf in the British motorcycle industry throughout the 'classic' period. Born of English parents in Lyons, France in 1906, he was the son of a tanner who at that time was working abroad. The Greeves family returned just prior to the start of World War 1. Not

*Manxman Dennis Craine rounds Quarterbridge on the Orpin RCS Silverstone during practice for the 1965 Lightweight Manx GP. Besides other modifications, the bike featured a Velocette 2LS front brake. He subsequently won the race at a record average 88.37 mph*

old enough for military service young Bert's first employment was as an apprentice to the Austin car company. But he soon left to work for Heenan and Froude, famous for their dynamometers. Then came a period prior to World War 2—and for much of the conflict—when together with a younger brother he ran a garage repair business in South London. Much of the influence from this move came from his love affair with motorcycles. Right from the day he rode (illegally!) his father's ancient 225 cc James, and the subsequent purchase of a new Norton CS1 in 1928, motorcycles had become a way of life. On the CS1 Bert not only travelled many thousands of

miles around Britain, but also took part in several trials.

Throughout the late 1930s the garage venture prospered. Then came the war, during which the partnership acted as small-scale sub-contractors doing machinery work for various government ministries. The garage was sold in 1945, and soon afterwards Bert made the most important move of his life—founding Invacar Ltd, to design and manu-facture invalid carriages. The idea for this venture came from his modification of a Villiers lawn mower engine, which he had fitted into a wheelchair belonging to his cousin. Derry Preston Cobb, who had been paralysed from birth.

The success of this project led to the Invacar com-pany which was set up in 1946 to cope with the high number of fellow sufferers, including many ex-servicemen who had been disabled during the war years.

Business boomed to such an extent that not only

was Invacar forced to move premises but subsequently regular expansions were needed.

With Invacar on a firm financial footing it should not perhaps have come as a surprise that Bert Greeves decided to build his own motorcycle. Then in May 1951 the motorcycle press published details of not one but two machines—a roadster and an off-roadster. These two prototypes were to lead, some two and a half years later, to an announcement in September 1953 that production was to begin of a series of Greeves motorcycles in roadster, trials and scrambles form.

Throughout the remainder of the 1950s and into the early 1960s the company, now based in Thundersley, Essex, built up an enviable reputation for its bikes, particularly in the off-road field where first Brian Stonebridge and later Dave Bickers continued to astound the bigger factories by their outstanding performances, even at the European Motocross Championship (the forerunner to the world series). In fact Bickers took the 250 cc title for the Essex marque in 1960 and again in 1961.

By 1962 the Greeves range listed 11 models—four roadsters and seven competition machines. All used Villiers engines and the proven I-beam alloy front frame member and leading-link front forks. In 1962

*Standard production 1965 RCS*

Bert Greeves also latched on to a completely new theme. Road racer Reg Everett had successfully campaigned a Greeves single in the 250 racing class at club and national level throughout the 1962 season. The subsequent adaptation of this home-built creation was to display Bert Greeves' strongest point: the ability to make full use of existing components which when developed properly could be turned into a commercial success. This was proved by the road racer.

Probably the most talked about exhibit at the 1962 Earls Court Show in November, the new racer from the Thundersley factory proved a wise move. Initially, simply named the Special (and later the Silverstone), the idea was to offer an inexpensive machine for the private owner.

Designated the 24RAS, the factory's prototype racer—as opposed to Everett's private machine—used a modified 246.3 cc (66 × 72 mm) Villiers 34A engine and was claimed to produce 25 bhp. A mere seven days after the official announcement of the Greeves production racer came news of a tie-up between the factory and the famous tuner Francis Beart. This agreement also included 1962 Senior Manx GP winner Joe Dunphy as rider.

The first batch of production RAS models began to be delivered to their owners in March 1963. These were all powered by the improved Villiers 36A

*Last Greeves production road racer, the 1968 RFS Oulton. This 344 cc, twin-exhaust-port single failed to match the success of the Silverstone. Only 21 were sold*

motor which now gave a full 30 bhp. The same month saw Tom Phillips give the new Greeves its first taste of glory with a win at Oulton Park. He was to maintain this form throughout the year to finish as ACU (British) Champion—a truly magnificent debut. This success was helped not only by the reliability and speed of the Greeves, but also the rider's skill. Another factor was the unreliability that year of the new Cotton and DMW racers or, more to the point, of their Villiers Starmaker engines.

Bert Greeves, however, was a realist and knew that this state of affairs wouldn't last, so to stay in front of the opposition it was necessary to create a new engine. During late 1963 and early 1964, the creative genius of Bert Greeves was hard at work. By March 1964 the world got a taste of things to come when the new Challenger motocross model was launched, and this was soon followed in the summer by the Mark 2 version of the Silverstone, the RBS. Both these machines featured the new engine. Cleverly this was based on the earlier Villiers unit, but totally redesigned for significantly more power. The bottom end was made to Bert Greeves' specification by Alpha, the crankpin was pressed into the

flywheel and an orthodox roller bearing con-rod was employed. The alloy head and cylinder were manufactured by Greeves who by then had their own foundry. These new components had a 50 per cent greater cooling area than the earlier Villiers 36A-based engine.

Bert realized that porting and exhaust shape were all important and devoted much of his time to ensuring that these were correct. For the road racing unit much of the actual work was carried out by two men, race shop mechanic Bob Mills and racing enthusiast Brian Woolley, the latter acting in a consultant capacity. In the end the road racing and motocross engines produced power characteristics suited to their own particular needs, this extended to the carburation too—an Amal Monobloc for the off-roader and a huge GP instrument for the Silverstone. For the transmission Greeves went to the Albion concern—a four-speed and brand new close-ratio unit respectively. The latter, fitted to the Silverstone, was to cause more than a few problems. The full story and much more detail on Greeves' racing history can be found in *Greeves* (Osprey Publishing) written jointly by Rob Carrick and myself.

Although not without their teething troubles, Bert Greeves' new babies made 1964 a year to remember, with perhaps Gordon Keith's 250 cc Manx Grand Prix victory the highlight. And to cap everything the Silverstone was voted 'Machine of

*Dr Gordon Blair (seated on 250 QUB watercooled twin) chatting to rider Brian Steenson, August 1969*

the Year' by readers of *Motor Cycle News*. The first time a road racer had been so honoured.

In 1965 the Silverstone continued where it had left off the previous year dominating the British short-circuit scene and again taking victory in September's Isle of Man races. This time with Manxman Dennis Craine aboard.

By 1966 the Silverstone was called the RDS, but

at least the foreign two-strokes, such as the water-cooled Bultaco TSS and Yamaha TD1B twin, were beginning to gain some reliability to add to their undoubted speed. In many ways the year can, in retrospect, be seen as the beginning of the end, not just for Greeves but for the British two-stroke in general. Although still competitive at club and national level in the hands of riders such as Bill Day, Trevor Burgess and Chas Mortimer, it was an Aermacchi, not a Greeves, that won the Lightweight Manx Grand Prix.

By 1967 things were looking grim. Yamaha had introduced the even quicker TDIC twin, whilst although there was a new Silverstone, the RFS, it was essentially the same bike, with only cosmetic changes.

No more Silverstones were produced after 1967, but the decision was taken to offer a bigger single, the 35RFS Oulton. This had stemmed from the success of the Brian Woolley-developed prototype ridden first by Trevor Burgess and then Mick Scruby. The Oulton had a capacity of 344 cc (80 × 65.5 mm) and its twin exhaust port engine produced around 40 bhp in standard production form. Sadly, the production version failed to repeat the performance of the original, and only 21 machines were actually manufactured. This is not to say that the Oulton was a complete flop because a handful of riders, notably Bob Stevenson, on Brian Woolley's model, extracted some truly excellent results from them. Stevenson even continued winning into the early 1970s.

There were other Greeves racers which were largely developments of the original Silverstone/Oulton theme—the 410 cc (85 × 72 mm) and 498 cc (91 × 76 mm), but these never left the prototype stage. Then there was the little-known 247 cc (54 × 54 mm) Alpha Centuri disc valve twin-engined bike, but again it was destined to remain only a prototype. (The engine was loaned by Alpha.)

*The Blair-designed 250 QUB twin engine*

*Brian Steenson on a 500 QUB during practice for the 1970 North West 200, the machine's first outing*

*Colin Seeley works on the 500 QUB single at Brands Hatch, September 1970*

And so the Greeves tarmac story came to an end, perhaps this was inevitable given Bert Greeves' partial retirement in 1968 from the company he had led for almost two decades.

But whatever might be said the fact remains that, judged on the quantities produced and the results gained, the Greeves Silverstone can lay claim to the title of Britain's most successful over-the-counter two-stroke racer of the classic era.

## QUB-Seeley

Dr Gordon Blair first began research into unsteady gas dynamics at Queens University, Belfast in 1959. But it was not to be until 1964 that he seriously considered constructing an actual engine to test the various theoretical procedures built up over the preceeding years. There was no real thought of actual racing participation then, only an academic experiment for further education amongst himself and his students.

A year later an approach was made by the BSA Group, via Mike Martin, for Dr Blair and his team to carry out work for the company into high specific output two-stroke engines and into the silencing of four-stroke motorcycle power units.

The financial support from BSA, in the way of grants over the next five years, helped Dr Blair's team to produce a single-cylinder 125 engine which was purely a test-bed exercise—this was completed in July 1967.

Two years later in June 1969 the first QUB (Queens University Belfast) racing machine was given its first testing. Claimed to produce 60–65 bhp, this 250 cc twin-cylinder two-stroke was stated by Dr Blair, 'To be the most potent 250 road racing engine ever built in Britain'.

The project was possible through the BSA support money and in addition to Dr Blair three others were involved, including post-graduate research student Mervyn Johnson who was responsible for making the entire set of engine components. A five-speed Albion gearbox was employed and it had toothed rubber belts, replacing the conventional chains to drive the intermediate pinion from the crankshaft. But its most interesting technical feature was a unique rotary valve system.

Fuel injection replaced the traditional carburettors, whilst the transistorized ignition system was a gift from Lucas. The rev-counter was made in the university's electrical department.

The engine assembly was mounted in a one-off Seeley spine frame, with the balance of the cycle parts coming from the same source.

Rider Ray McCullough was not only one of Ulster's leading stars of the period but also a university technician, thus making him an ideal choice.

In an interview at the time of the launch of the 250 QUB twin, Dr Blair commented: 'Gone are the days of the hacksaw. Computer calculation played a big part in the design of such parts as the cylinder head and exhaust system. Our aim here is to follow the theoretical design of gas dynamics, and to achieve high specific outputs from small two-stroke engines on a theoretical basis.'

Although McCullough did much of the initial testing, it was up-and-coming star Brian Steenson who was enlisted to race it. Although fast it proved extremely fragile. In an attempt to cure this various modifications were made, including changing the fuel-injection system to conventional carburettors. But ultimately all this was to prove of no avail. Then came an engine which was born of a conversation between Dr Blair and Colin Seeley. Worried by the ever-increasing costs of his ageing Matchless G50-based ohc single, Seeley prompted Dr Blair to consider an alternative. And so the idea of a lightweight 500 with enough power to make it competitive was created, capable of winning at national and even international level.

Dr Blair reasoned that in racing, power—sheer brake horsepower—wasn't the be all and end all, as even the mighty Honda factory had discovered with their evil handling 500 four of the late 1960s. What really counted was the power-to-weight ratio and the ability to transmit this power on to the tarmac. Dr Blair's problem was that of providing adequate power for the weight of the engine unit. He reasoned that 60 bhp from an engine weighing 50 lb would be a good starting-point.

The low weight and the intended use of the machine, essentially a private owner's bike, ruled out four-strokes or multi-cylinder designs. These would either have been very complicated in order to produce enough power or they would simply have been too heavy. What, Dr Blair reasoned, could be more simple than a single-cylinder two-stroke?

At this stage (summer 1969) an engine specification was computed: bore and stroke 91 × 76 mm giving a capacity of 495 cc and a bore/stroke ratio of

*First track test of the new single-cylinder, two-stroke Royal Enfield by John Hartle at Oulton Park, 16 March 1964*

*Royal Enfield GP5 chassis. Note the low, full duplex frame, leading-link forks and Girling rear shocks*

1.2, which Dr Blair considered to be the optimum for the type of engine. The primary (crankcase) compression ratio was 'very high' whilst the secondary ratio was very nearly 15 : 1 using a squish head with a squish band of half the bore area. It should be pointed out that the effective or trapped compression ratio, measured from the top of the exhaust port, was less than 8 : 1. The piston was slightly domed the crown having a 130 mm radius, in order to direct the gas flow up into the combustion space. The porting was controlled by the piston and was quite conventional apart from the fact that multiple transfer ports were used, but all transfer ports had identical timing. The Amal concern produced a special 42 mm Concentric carburettor which employed a remote float chamber. The engine was lubricated by a petroil mixture, using Castrol R40 in a 16 : 1 ratio. If this seems dated compared to the far less 'smokey' ratios used today, not only was oil technology less advanced 20 years ago but Dr Blair stated in tests that no noticeable effect on power output came from using ratios from 16 to 32 : 1.

On its first test during the spring of 1970, the new engine weighed in at 52 lb and produced 61 bhp—very close to the original target figures. As with the 250 QUB twin, the 500 single employed a Seeley chassis and running gear. The new QUB-Seeley was raced for the first time in Ulster during May 1970, with Ray McCullough aboard. Soon it chalked up its first victory, but at the cost of problems with reliability. Colin Seeley later admitted to 'piston, small-end and transmission failures'. Another insider recently confirmed these problems, which he stated 'were never fully overcome and the reason why the machine never entered production'. This particular source also stated that primary chains (duplex) and pistons were the real bugbears. Another was power loss—at the crankshaft a true 60 bhp was obtained, but by the time this reached the rear wheel it was down to 52 bhp. Had the QUB-Seeley been offered for sale it would no doubt have featured gear primary drive. In an attempt to improve reliability the original points set-up was ditched in favour of a lighter fully transistorized circuit which also reduced the risk of failure with no moving parts.

Another reason why the project never made it was Colin Seeley's choice of riders—for example both Dave Croxford and Alan Barnett were first and foremost four-stroke men and both loathed the unfamiliar 'stroker. Even so, Barnett was quoted at the time as saying, 'It's the fastest 500 I've ridden with excellent steering capabilities'.

It was only back in Ulster that the QUB-Seeley shone (when it didn't break!) McCullough was the only rider who could make full use of the machine and this he proved by his excellent results on the bike in the early 1970s.

# Royal Enfield GP5

With its famous slogan 'Built like a gun', the Redditch-based Royal Enfield company could trace its history back to the middle of the nineteenth century. Its first two-wheelers (pedal cycles) were produced during the 1880s. Soon guns and motor-cycles were to be added. Although one of the British industry's founder members, an Enfield didn't compete in the TT until the mid 1930s and the company became more well known for its off-road exploits. During World War 2 Enfield produced thousands of WD machines.

It was the successes of the mechanically simple Greeves Silverstone which prompted the Enfield management, headed by ex-TT winner Leo Daven-

Above
*GP5 cylinder barrel—note bridged port*

Below
*A 1½ in. Amal GP carburettor dominates the GP5 engine. The contact-breakers are housed behind the small crankcase cover*

port, into developing their own machine, but orders were that it had to be better! The GP5 originally started life with one of the new Villiers Starmaker road race engines mounted in a specially produced Reynolds frame. The Starmaker engine, with its 68 × 68 mm bore and stroke and 30 bhp at 7500 rpm, seemed to be just what Enfield were looking for. This was in 1963 and with concentrated development the new GP5 hit the headlines with its official launch in early 1964.

However, all was not well with the new silver and red machine and despite the combined talents of race manager Geoff Duke and top star of the day, John Hartle, results were difficult to come by. From its first race at Oulton Park, at Easter in 1964, the Starmaker-engined prototype was doomed, but it did lay down the general arrangement on which future GP5s were modelled. Equipped with Reynolds leading-link forks, Reynolds 531 constructed frame and 7 in. Enfield single leading-shoe front brake, the GP5 was on its way.

Enfield, by then owned by E. & H. P. Smith, soon called upon the services of other companies within the group to assist with the project. Frank Cutler and Alpha Bearings provided one of their 66 × 72 mm racing crankshaft and crankcase assemblies and Albion supplied their HG5 five-speed gearbox and clutch. The only thing which stopped Enfield producing an in-house engine was the lack of a suitable two-stroke tuning wizard.

This is where Hermann Meier comes on the scene. Working in Birmingham for Matt Holder and the Scott concern he was soon lured away to become development chief responsible for the new Grand Prix 5 racer. What he found was the basis of a strong and reliable engine unit and all that was needed was to find that elusive extra few horsepower.

In 1964, for the Manx Grand Prix, he produced his first prototype that can be related to future production models. But it was still fitted with the rather unreliable HG5 gearbox and a standard Alpha 72 mm stroke crankshaft/crankcase assembly. The new machine did, however, incorporate several new features such as a Reynolds duplex frame, Avon fairing, Oldani rear brake (replacing the previous British Hub Company unit) and a 60 mm engine/gearbox spacer, which was Meier's attempt to reduce heat pick-up from the transmission by allowing cooler more dense gas to enter the cylinder and therefore increase output.

The machine was ridden by Dennis Craine, in the 1964 Manx GP, and to ensure he finished it was fitted with an alloy 5-gallon seat tank unit. See-

ing photographs of the day it was hard to believe that the little tank was able to hold three gallons let alone five, but it was the seat that held the secret. The fuel was carried not only in the tank but in the seat as well, in fact, Dennis was sitting on approximately two gallons of it.

After several mainland short-circuit races, piloted by none other than the evergreen Percy Tait, the GP5 was whisked away for a winter of intense development. The engine now received its close finned five-port cylinder which produced an immediate 32 bhp at 8000 rpm. This encouraging result was later increased to 34 bhp at 8000 rpm and in fact was the final state of tune when Enfield went into limited production with the first batch of GP5 racers.

Assisted by competition shop foreman Charlie Rogers, Meier changed the HG5 gearbox for the latest five-speed barrel cam Albion unit, which was manufactured to Enfield's requirements. Alpha produced a special crankcase/crankshaft assembly which was needed to accommodate the latest 9 in. diameter five-port cylinder. Ignition was effected by a simple 6-volt battery coil arrangement and the gearbox was driven by a Reynolds duplex primary chain. But it was the cylinder and its porting arrangement that made the new prototype really fly.

Walter Kaaden had started the ball rolling in the mid 1950s when he added an additional port to the rear of an MZ cylinder (both Zündapp and Levis used similar ideas on roadsters in pre-war days). This was not in search of additional power but reliability. Fed by a hole in the rear of the piston he hoped that the cooling effect of the incoming charge would extend the life of the small-end and add some reliability to the fragile and overworked piston. It worked and worked well. However, by adding an extra port he not only increased reliability but found to his surprise a dramatic increase in power.

Meier's version was applied to the piston-ported Enfield but instead of one additional port he added two, and these were not just fed by communicating holes in the piston! The new ports ran alongside the main pair of transfer ports and were fed directly from the crankcases, but searching for increased reliability from the 66 mm Hepolite piston, Meier machined two slots (one each side) just above the gudgeon pin boss, so forcing a flow of gas under the piston crown and over the bronze small-end bearing. The new smaller transfer ports were angled upwards and rearward at 45 degrees—a layout later seen on the first true five-port Yamaha, the 1969 TD2.

Apart from the Enfield name, the extended ribbing and the wider front stud spacing, the new

*Royal Enfield works rider Percy Tait competing in a wet Hutchinson 100, Silverstone, 17 August 1965. He finished third behind the Yamaha works pair of Mike Duff and Phil Read*

crankcases were dimensionally the same as the previous Alpha units. The fins were added to satisfy Meier's obsession with crankcase cooling and the stud positions were shifted to accommodate the wide bridged flat topped exhaust port in the newly developed cylinder.

The rest of the machine was in fact similar to the £350 production version but there were subtle differences. The oiling system of the works machine didn't rely on a petroil mix alone, but had been adapted to accommodate a Suzuki type crankshaft oil-feed system. This simple, but effective, layout relied on negative crankcase pressure to suck oil from a frame mounted tank, through a non-return valve and into the alloy caged roller main bearings. From there the oil passed out into the crankcase and that's where centrifugal force took over. Caught by a machined groove, in the side of the 111 mm diameter flywheels the oil was given only one way to escape and this was through a small hole in the hollow crankpin. This in turn was drilled to allow the oil to pass directly on to the big-end roller bearing.

*The 344 cc, aircooled Scott. This racing twin first appeared in 1964*

Other differences between the factory machine and the production models were restricted to cycle parts, with needle roller leading-link fork pivots and eccentric cam rear chain adjustment, but on the whole they were very much alike.

When the 250 cc GP5 reached the hands of private owners, in 1965, most were pleasantly surprised as the new machines proved markedly quicker than the Greeves Silverstone or the Villiers-engined DMW Hornet. However, the GP5, with its fabricated leading-link forks, was susceptible to surface conditions and provided somewhat neutral handling (my own views from having ridden a production GP5 in 1966). It must be said though that works rider Percy Tait rated the roadholding as 'excellent'. With conventional front forks the damping oil viscosity could be varied, as could the spring rate, but the GP5 was equipped with a pair of unique extra-long Girling gas-oil units which resisted modification.

Percy Tait's factory prototype was now produc-

ing 37 bhp and was as quick as the best, but indifferent results only detracted from the machine's public appeal. Not that Percy or the others didn't win, they did and riders such as Mick Scruby, Gordon Keith and George Ward romped home to victory on many a circuit.

By the end of the 1965 season the factory machine was as fast as anything 'Made in Britain' in the quarter-litre category. Meier wanted to press on but Enfield didn't want to spend any extra money on development so he quit—taking a job with Kawasaki in North America. This was to signal the end for the Redditch racer.

GP5 production soldiered on in 1966 but little had changed except the colour scheme which was now a black frame with red seat and tank unit. The price tag, which had been upped to £450, put it £65 above the Greeves Silverstone and only £100 short of the rapidly developing Yamaha twin. So the future wasn't that rosy for the GP5, in fact, the machine ceased to be produced in January 1967.

When Enfield finally threw in the towel the complete competition shop and all it contained was purchased in March 1967 by Cowies of Sunderland who proceeded to finish a couple of bikes but in the main sold the bits at knockdown prices to special builders. Many a Yamaha engine found its way into a GP5 frame, but very few were fitted with the original leading-link forks—there must be a moral there somewhere.

The built-on-a-budget racer could have been better if Hermann Meier had been allowed to stay and when you think what he and his team achieved in that one-year development period it is quite remarkable. But what happened to the GP5?

Sadly most seem to have disappeared. It is only very occasionally that the odd bike turns up at a classic club meeting. This is a great pity as it prevents enthusiasts viewing what must stand out as one of the quickest and sleekest British 250 racers of the 1960s.

*Barry Scully with the Scott at Oulton Park, 1966*

## Scott

A famous name from the vintage and veteran period, a Scott first made its appearance at the TT in 1909, and it is a marque bathed in history. Alfred Scott could well be described as Britain's leading exponent of the two-stroke engine in the early days. But by 1964 the famous old company was in fresh hands—owned by the Matt Holder-controlled Aerco Jigs and Tools company, based in Birmingham.

As no new racer had appeared from the famous marque since the 1930s, it came as a shock when a totally new machine made its bow in June 1964.

This was very much a prototype, with its 344 cc square dimension 60.3 × 60.3 mm inclined parallel twin engine, with a 180 degree crankshaft designed by Aerco design engineer, Bill Reid, as a potential replacement for the now ageing traditional Scott 600 cc Flying Squirrel.

Also associated with the project were Hermann Meier, Brian Woolley and Brian Bulmer. The last had

*Peter Inchley with the Bultaco-framed Villiers special, Snetterton, 10 April 1966*

been responsible for the full loop lightweight frame which featured a single front downtube and duplex rear and top rails.

For the first time, except for the short-lived Swift roadster of 1958, Scott broke away from the use of the deflector-type piston. The Y-alloy pistons of Bill Reid's design had very slightly domed crowns rising into squish combustion chambers framed by deeply spigoted four-stud fitting cylinder heads, with no head gaskets employed.

The cylinder barrels, like the heads, were in light alloy with close-pitch fins and cast-in Chromindium liners. The engine was designed to run at around 10.5:1 compression ratio, and it was ultimately hoped that it would push out around 45 bhp and be capable of speeds of up to 125 mph.

The one-piece crankcase housed a forged two-piece crankshaft. The crankshaft halves were assembled in a taper with a key and key-way, whilst the traditional Scott type central flywheel was locked

up by a long Allen bolt. For racing use, a considerable amount of the centre flywheel was machined away, making it virtually no more than a rigid flange joining the shafts together.

The machine was supposed to make its racing debut at the Southern 100 in July 1964 but during testing at an airfield location in England a piston seized and the plan was abandoned. Brian Woolley recalls that a total of four prototype engines were built but he quit the team in 1965 after his rider, Trevor Burgess, said that 'it didn't handle' (not helped by an 'elastic' swinging arm which distorted so much that the chain jumped off the sprockets!). It also had continual engine seizures. But the 350 Scott did garner some early success, including a new course record for the Barbon Hill Climb and eighth in the Irish Temple 100 road races.

Although Barry Scully stuck to the Scott throughout its racing life he must have been a man of considerable patience because it suffered one problem after another—although occasionally it put in a good performance, it best years being 1966 and 1968.

This probably accounts for the reason why plans to build a production version in early 1966 did not materialize. The price of this small quantity, hand-built job would have been around £600, which for a 350 twin-cylinder two-stroke was expensive.

Finally, tiring of the aircooled 350, the Scott management commissioned a 500 in the late 1960s. This first appeared in 1969, but was heavily modified for the 1970 season. The rider was still Barry Scully. The engine, although still a twin, was now watercooled and had a bore and stroke of 70 × 64 mm and revved to 10,000 rpm. Primary drive was by gear (the aircooled 350 was by chain) to a five-speed Albion box. The engine was looked after by Brian Bulmer, but the services of Brian Woolley had been sought for the design and construction of the exhaust system. Woolley also personally cut the ports in the cylinder. An unusual feature of the engine was its five-bearing crankshaft, with one bearing on each side of each cylinder, plus an outrigger to support the primary gear. The cooling system included a pump driven by a rubber V-belt on the end of the crankshaft, a radiator, and a header tank in front of the forks.

Other details included a diaphragm clutch and 38 mm Spanish-built Amal Concentric carburettors. Unfortunately this machine proved little better than the ill-fated 350 and the whole Scott racing project was finally abandoned.

## Villiers Special/AJS Starmaker

Sired by the single-cylinder Starmaker scrambles engine, the road racing variant made its public bow in October 1962, as the prime mover for the Cotton Telstar.

When it entered production the following February it was fitted with twin Amal Monobloc carburettors working on the primary-secondary system. But conventional carburation, with a single Amal 1½ in. 3GP2 instrument was soon adopted. This early development work on Bernard Hooper's design boosted power output from 25 bhp at 6500 rpm to 28 bhp at 7500 rpm.

Improved breathing through a new cylinder and head in 1964 lifted the output to a claimed 30 bhp at 7500 rpm. The associated redesign of the exhaust system also played an important part.

One of the early problems experienced was big-end failure caused through over-revving.

When conceived the Starmaker was produced with a four-speed gearbox—and the production version always employed this—Villiers saying that cost was the arbiter.

*Inchley leads Neil Kelly (Royal Enfield) on his way to a record-breaking victory in the Southern 100 during the evening of 16 July 1966*

*Starmaker AJS developed from the Inchley special. Hopes of sales success were stopped in their tracks by the performance of the latest Yamaha production racers*

But it soon became evident that the top riders needed more ratios to extract maximum power. With this in mind, Villiers laid out a six-speed box. Designed by John Favill in February 1964, this was used in the works development racer which Villiers engineer Peter Inchley created the same year.

Inchley's machine employed a standard Bultaco TSS frame and running gear with one of the Wolverhampton-built Starmaker engines and Villiers six-speed box. There were no snags in fitting the engine-gearbox unit into the Spanish frame. Fabricating mounting plates and offsetting the unit enough to get the chainline right were straight-

forward problems. This left Inchley free to concentrate on the engine development.

The Starmaker 247 cc (68 × 68 mm) used aluminium alloy for the crankcases, cylinder head, chaincases and gearbox shell.

An austenitic-iron liner was spun-cast integral with the light-alloy cylinder muff. A 12:1 compression piston had a large diameter gudgeon pin to assist heat transfer away from the crown, narrow anti-flutter rings were employed.

The crankshaft was carried on two roller bearings and one needle assembly. Connected to the timing-side shaft by a nylon coupling, a subsidiary 'main-shaft' carried the contact breaker cam. This outrigger shaft was unaffected by whip and there was consequently no variation in the make-and-break of the contact points. Dry weight of the 1964 Inchley

Villiers Special was 203 lb. Inchley's engine modifications were more subtle. The inlet port was larger than the stock Starmaker's, so were the transfer ports and the exhaust was an exceptionally wide, bridged affair that might well have been modelled on the Dartford tunnel! Despite this, the engine was still fed by the production engine's 1½-in. Amal GP carburettor and remained a conventional three-port loop-scavenge design. By taking third place behind the works Hondas of Mike Hailwood and Stuart Graham in the 1966 TT, Inchley clearly demonstrated that the Villiers factory had the makings of a truly competitive production racer.

At the time of the 1966 TT Inchley's motor was credited with 35 bhp at 8500 rpm and was noticeably quicker than the standard unit. However, I suspect that the truth of the matter was that the production engines fell short of the factory's 30 bhp claim. . . and Inchley's was in fact putting out 37–38 bhp, which would be more in keeping with its 15 mph advantage.

The big merger took place in 1967, and while everyone concerned was trying to fend off the inevitable, Dennis Poore finally captured the AMC and Villiers factories. So where did this leave Peter Inchley and his Starmaker 250? As Chairman of the Norton-Villiers/Manganese Bronze empire, Poore boasted of his affection for road racing and as the AJS 250 had shown promise, it would therefore be developed further, put into limited production and later offered to the public for general consumption. So AJS went through the motions of commissioning a Reynolds frame and replacing most items except wheels and engine with components of their own manufacture. Finally, in May 1967 a new and purposeful AJS appeared looking every inch a winner.

The new 15½ lb Reynolds 531 tubing frame consisted of a 2¼ in. main spine with 1 in. duplex bottom loop. The little Ajay also sported a new tank and seat design, but just for the TT, an additional 1¼-gallon fuel tank was located behind the engine. The engine remained virtually unchanged, with its close-finned cylinder, six-speed gearbox and duplex chain-driven diaphragm clutch. However, the bike now featured an all-new exhaust system with a greatly reduced tail-pipe diameter.

The development of a new machine should always be a low-key affair, yet in true British tradition Norton-Villiers and the press generated an aura of hype around the machine which rapidly dissipated when Inchley and the new machine parted company at its Mallory Park debut. The 1967 TT was equally disastrous, for Inchley's engine locked solid just after a fuel stop. Yet this didn't deter Dennis Poore—by now with the bit firmly between his teeth—who promptly announced a price for the production version: £418.

With hindsight we know that, due to lack of sales, Cotton had already halted the production of the Telstar in 1966, as had DMW with their Hornet racer and Royal Enfield with the GP5. Only Greeves managed to soldier on until the spring of 1967, which is when poor sales halted the production of the Silverstone. So why was Norton-Villiers apparently going full steam ahead into an ever-decreasing market with a rapidly ageing machine that they knew wasn't going to sell? One reason may have been that the public loves a good story about an all-British machine, especially one that comes from a stable that included such illustrious names as AJS and Norton.

Nevertheless, the little two-stroke on which Peter Inchley had worked so hard never made it into production. However, one of the new development bikes managed to escape the maw of the scrapyard and recently surfaced at an auction where it was expected to fetch the princely sum of £2000. Fortunately, and against all odds, this machine has survived relatively intact and bears a remarkable resemblance to its original appearance. Considering its final demise as a pre-production prototype was steeped in political confusion, it represents a unique slice of British motorcycle racing history.

# 11
# Velocette

Besides Norton and AJS, what other British manufacturer has won a road racing World Championship? The answer is Velocette. And the relatively small Hall Green, Birmingham factory managed not one, but two in a brief two-year period of glory at the highest level in 1949 and 1950.

Velocette machines had been competing in the TT since 1913 and in 1926 Alec Bennett really put the name on the map when he won the Junior TT on one of their new overhead-camshaft machines. This design, which was to be the forerunner of the famous KTT model, went on to achieve numerous Continental victories and win two more Junior TTs before

being eclipsed by the factory Rudge and Norton machines.

A Velocette comeback started in 1934 when Walter Rusk finished third in the Senior TT on a larger capacity version of the 350. Then for three years in succession, 1936–8, that truly great master, Stanley Woods, piloted a Velocette into second place in the Senior TT, creating in the process some of the most exciting finishes ever seen. In the 350 cc category the cammy Velos were even more successful, for the works machines won countless events at home and abroad including the 1938 and 1939 Junior TTs.

On the production front the first over-the-counter KTT racers appeared in very limited

*The 1947 Velocette 349 cc KTT Mark VIII*

*Peter Goodman with his KTT after winning the 350 cc race at Scarborough, 1 May 1947*

quantity during 1928, but the following year a considerable number were produced, aided by another Junior TT victory.

Design changes took place as the years passed, the first of real significance was in 1932 when a redesigned cylinder head appeared, fitted with hairpin valve springs.

Hairpins were found to be necessary with engine revolutions increasing above 6000 rpm. Other improvements included the employment of a 14 mm spark plug and a more compact camshaft oil-pump. Another change was in the material of the cylinder head to a bi-metal aluminium-bronze component. Finally, the frame was modified to carry a larger 3½-gallon tank, and a new four-speed gearbox was fitted.

With all these changes the KTT was marketed as the Mark IV.

Next to appear was the Mark V in 1935 and this had many improvements as a direct result of experiences gained from the works machines. The new cradle frame was used, together with the lubrication system in which oil was supplied to the big-end, top bevel gears and camshaft through a set of metered jets.

During 1936 and 1937 the KTT model was not produced, but in 1938 the Mark VII made its bow. This featured the vast majority of the latest works machine's features, except that the engine had more rounded finning and it still employed a rigid frame (a swinging-arm type had been introduced on the works models from 1936 onwards).

On the eve of World War 2, Velocette decided to again update its KTT and so the definitive Mark VIII was born. Its most noticeable feature was the works type swinging-arm rear suspension which was a first on a production racer. Employing a 10.9 : 1 compression ratio the Mark VIII was capable of over 110 mph—a magnificent performance for its time.

*Bob Foster, second in the 1948 Junior TT*

As proof of the machine's popularity, Velocette machines took 25 of the first 35 places in the 1939 Junior TT.

The same year the company produced a very special works machine. This was a supercharged vertical twin of 496 cc (68 × 68.25 mm) with unit construction and shaft drive. Nicknamed the 'Roarer' it was intended to challenge the continental marques which had wrested superiority from Britain. But after showing great promise, when Stanley Woods practised on it on the Isle of Man, its development had to be shelved in September 1939 with the outbreak of war.

After the hostilities had ended the twin could not be used as the FIM banned superchargers, and in

any case the company's first task was to resume peacetime production and help the nation back on the road to recovery with its drive for exports.

When the TT was resumed in 1947 Velocette responded with Bob Foster winning the Junior event. Not only this, but Velocettes also finished second and third, David Whitworth setting the fastest lap at 81.61 mph. Velocettes also won the Dutch TT and Swiss GP.

In 1948 the former Norton star Freddie Frith (who had joined the team a year earlier only to break a collarbone in the TT) got back to winning ways by taking the Junior TT at an average speed of 81.45 mph, with the fastest lap of 82.45 mph. Meanwhile, production KSS models won the Junior Clubmans race.

Frith went on to win the Ulster GP, Bob Foster

the Belgian, Ken Bills the Dutch and David Whitworth came second in the Swiss GP, which was the only classic which Velocette failed to win that year.

Then it was 1949 and the first year of the new 'official' World Championship Series. For this the Velocette competitions department brought out new 350 and 500 cc singles with dohc cylinder heads. The smaller engine displaced 348.3 cc (74 × 81 mm). In the five-round series Freddie Frith carried off the 350 cc world title in convincing fashion with five wins and five new lap records! After this success Frith retired and opened up a motorcycle business in his native Grimsby. The 500 was far less successful with only a third place (Ernie Lyons) in the Senior TT and a fifth place in the Swiss GP by Frith to show by the season's end.

*Marseilles, France, 19 March 1950. Velocette KTT rider Tommy Wood after his victorious ride in the Circuit de Marseilles race*

In 1950 it was left to Bob Foster to carry on the winning sequence and he retained the 350 cc World Championship for the Birmingham company, with victories in Belgium, Holland and Ulster. Other team members that year were Reg Armstrong and Bill Lomas. Strangely, Foster retired after winning his title—like Frith to concentrate on his own business, this time at Parkstone in Dorset. (He was the British Guzzi agent in the early 1950s.)

For 1951 the factory astounded many by introducing a new double-knocker 250, but against the Italian Moto Guzzi horizontal single it simply wasn't

fast enough. Even with riders of the calibre of Graham, Sandford and Lomas the double world championship-winning 350 wasn't good enough to match the latest Norton and AJS machines.

The final production KTTs were manufactured in 1949 and in non-championship events they could still be race winners, as was proved many, many times around the world in the next few years.

The last season of factory involvement was in 1952, and from then on Velocette's fortunes faded. This process continued until 1956 when the Viper and Venom high-performance sports roadsters appeared on the scene and began to prove successful in clubman type racing. Events such as the newly introduced Thruxton Nine Hour race (see Chapter 13) and the Clubmans TT proved the machine's forte.

But most famous of all the achievements made by the sporting ohv Venom came in March 1961 when

a team of eight riders (two Englishmen and six Frenchmen) smashed the 12- and 24-hour records in the 500, 750 and 1000 cc solo classes. The average speed for the shorter distance was 104.66 mph and for the longer, 100.05 mph. The records were set on the bumpy steeply banked Montlhéry speed bowl near Paris.

Specially prepared at the factory, the machine was essentially a production 499 cc Venom with a megaphone exhaust and factory Veeline fairing. Top gear was raised from the standard 4.87 : 1 to 3.98 : 1 by substituting a 22-tooth final drive sprocket for the usual 18-tooth component.

In the world of production machine racing the Venom continued to do well, including victories in its class in the Thruxton events, now called the 500

**Above left**
*Charlie Hurst, winner of the 1953 350 cc Natal 100, South Africa*

**Below left**
*Engine details of F. C. A. Rutherford's Mark VIII, Manx GP, 1952*

**Right**
*The record-breaking Venom engine being inspected after it had successfully completed the 24-hour stint*

**Below**
*Georges Monneret on the specially prepared 499 cc Venom, which became the first motorcycle to average over 100 mph for 24 hours—100.05 mph at Montlhéry, near Paris, 18–19 March 1961*

The 1964 Thruxton 500-mile 500 cc class-winning Venom, which was piloted by Howard German (shown) and Alan Harris

Superbly crafted Seymour Velocette/Metisse—a regular sight in the late 1960s and early 1970s

Mile Race. In this, two notable entrants emerged: Geoff Dodkin and the Goldhawk Road, Shepherds Bush concern of L. E. Stevens, headed by Reg Orpin. The latter also built a Clubman's type machine for open events in the mid 1960s but it didn't prove particularly successful.

Then in 1965 came the Thruxton model, the factory's response to numerous pleas for a machine of even greater performance. This soon established an excellent reputation and is much sought-after by collectors today.

Other projects are worthy of mention. The first is the Jim Lee Velocette which Mick Grant began his racing career with, while the immaculate Seymour Velocette was created by the Oxfordshire enthusiast and gifted engineer Ralph Seymour and, finished in British racing green, employed a special Rickman Metisse chassis. Finally, Ilford dealers BMG built a special Venom equipped with a desmodromic cylinder head.

Today both the pukka racing KTT and various pushrod-based Venom/Thruxton conversions can be seen at either vintage or classic club race meetings to remind us just what an important part these traditional black and gold British singles played in motorcycling history.

# 12
# Vincent HRD

Founded in 1924, by Howard Raymond Davies, a rider of considerable note, the HRD company gained almost overnight success when its creator won the 1925 Senior TT with a JAP-engined machine of his own design.

But although Freddie Dixon won the Junior TT in 1927 on another HRD, the company was up to its eyeballs in debt. And soon afterwards went into voluntary liquidation.

On to the scene came Philip Vincent who, financed by his father to the tune of £30,000, took over the ailing concern in June 1928 to form the Vincent HRD Company Ltd.

*George Brown in race-winning form at Oliver's Mount, Scarborough, in the late 1940s*

Based in Stevenage the first Vincent motorcycle, the forerunner of the world famous series of V-twins, was unique only in the construction of its frame, as all the other components were bought in from outside suppliers. But even so the frame showed much original thought and incorporated a top tube which could be lengthened or shortened, enabling its designer to experiment with various rake angles of the steering head. But the most innovative was the rear springing, and although there had been sprung frames before, the Vincent creation was far in excess of the majority.

It was not until 1934, however, that Vincent got around to producing machines with engines designed 'in-house'.

Besides two production roadsters, there was also

*The 1950 Senior TT saw the experienced Ken Bills finish in 12th spot at an average speed of 83.79 mph*

a pukka racing job, the TT model. All three were powered by a 499 cc (84 × 90 mm) single-cylinder ohv engine, in which the camshaft was placed as high as possible, thereby reducing reciprocating weight to the bare minimum (a similar method was used by the Italian Parilla company in the post-war period). The design was the joint work of Philip Vincent and Phil Irving.

All three models were shown for the first time at the 1934 Motor Cycle Show at Olympia, and as Roy Harper reveals in his excellent book *Vincent Vee-Twins* (Osprey Publishing) at that stage none of the new engines had even been fired up in anger! It was not to be until the following year that the company got around to actually putting the new bikes into production.

In the 1935 Senior TT Vincent HRD machines, fitted with the new powerplant, came home seventh, ninth, 11th, 12th and 13th to display excellent reliability. The leading rider was none other than the 'Cheltenham Flyer', Jack Williams, later to win fame as the prime mover in the development of the AJS 7R and Matchless G50 racing machines at AMC. Another famous figure who rode Vincent HRD

machines during this period was BMW and AMC racer Jock West.

In 1936 one of the Vincent HRD singles finished eighth in the Senior TT, but the three others entered all retired. But perhaps more important to the company's future was the appearance of a prototype V-twin. Dubbed 'the plumber's nightmare' the Series A Rapide made its entry into the world in October that year. During the machine's first trials it clocked 108 mph, making it faster than the rival Brough Superior SS100.

In 1938 the factory built a special racing model of the Series A Rapide. Both used a 998 cc (84 × 90 mm) 47.5-degree angle V-twin engine which employed cylinder barrels and heads of the same design as the 500 single.

On 2 July the works V-twin racer appeared in the Dublin 100 at Phoenix Park, Dublin. This took part in the 24-lap handicap event. Ridden by local rider Manliff Barrington (later to win fame as a works Moto Guzzi rider), the 998 cc Stevenage model soon proved its worth by upping the lap record by no less than 6 mph, to 86.67 mph and eventually finishing second—even though it had been heavily handicapped.

Later, Vincent's chief tester, Ginger Woods, rode the machine at the August Bank Holiday Donington

Park meeting. After being left at the start Woods proceeded to thunder around the Derbyshire circuit at a remarkable rate of knots to shatter the lap record before the clutch cried enough.

With war clouds gathering at an even quickening pace, thoughts of racing had to be put to one side and the mind concentrated on the national effort.

After the conflict the Vincent HRD concern were fortunate to be able to move into a new 42,000 sq. ft factory (still in Stevenage) during early 1946. This was in addition to the existing facilities which were retained.

Shortly afterwards in April 1946 came the first news of a new Rapide V-twin. The Series B was a major redesign of the concept—although it still retained the bore and stroke dimensions of the original pre-war engine.

Production of the Series 2 Rapide began in the autumn of 1946 and in technical terms it differed from the Series 1 machine in several ways. For a start the clutch was completely new and the angle of the cylinders increased to 50 degrees, thus eliminating the front downtube. The wheelbase was reduced and the top frame tube was also eliminated and in its place was a one-piece all-welded 16-gauge steel

*Pat Walsh's 499 cc Vincent, Senior Manx Grand Prix, 1952*

oil tank, which forever after became a hallmark of the company's motorcycles. The engine was also redesigned with many alterations in specifications. Unfortunately, space precludes their inclusion, but in any case they are amply covered in Roy Harper's book.

In January 1947 the news came of an innovation for the 1947 TT Series—the first to be held post-war of a new four-lap event, the Clubman's TT. Not only this but the exciting prospect of seeing the Stevenage V-twins race around the legendary $37\frac{3}{4}$-mile Mountain circuit, as the upper capacity limit was set at 1000 cc. Unfortunately, the organizers later did an about face, the result being that machines were restricted to 500 cc.

For 1948 a more sporting version of the Rapide was introduced for fast road work *and* clubman's racing, the Black Shadow, which could be recognized by it black outer engine covers, not to mention its searing acceleration.

In 1948 the 1000 cc machines were finally allowed in the Clubman's TT. *The Motor Cycle* race report said it all: 'Vincent HRDs Outpaced All Rivals in Senior—J. D. Daniels the Winner at 80.51 mph'.

There were no less than 11 of the 998 cc Stevenage V-twins in the race and George Brown had led for much of the race, only to run short of fuel on the final circuit. He eventually pushed in to finish

*Nathan Smith on a 998 Vincent HRD, Parkhill 120, Durban, South Africa, 1 August 1949*

sixth. For several years afterwards Vincent dominated the 1000 cc Clubman's race in much the same way that the BSA Gold Stars did in the other classes.

George Brown was by then already some way towards his eventual legendary status amongst the Vincent fans, with a number of special Vincents, including the famous *Gunga Din*. This and other outstanding performances by the 998 cc V-twin around the world convinced Philip Vincent to market a pukka racing machine. This was called the Series C Black Lightning and made its debut at the 1948 Earls Court Show. Compared to the Black Shadow, the Black Lightning boasted higher lift cams, a steel idler timing gear, $1\frac{5}{32}$ in. Amal TT carburettors, a Lucas manually operated racing magneto, a pair of 2 in. bore straight through exhaust pipes, alloy wheel rims, tacho and a choice of compression ratio up to

a maximum of 13 : 1. The gearbox was also modified to give a quicker change. In addition, both the front and rear suspension were modified.

In 1948 the American rider Rollie Free also became the first man to ride an unsupercharged motorcycle at 150 mph.

The following year saw the introduction of a higher performance single, which was marketed as the Series C Grey Flash. It was available in three guises: as a pukka racer, as a sports roadster with full lighting equipment and silencer or as roadster supplied with racing equipment for easy transfer into racing trim.

The Grey Flash was tuned to Black Lightning specification and to live up to its name the tank and frame components were painted in grey-green to distinguish the model from the standard Comet roadster. Weighing 330 lb and costing £300 plus purchase tax, the Grey Flash pumped out 35 bhp at 6200 rpm.

*Awesome Black Lightning racer, 1951*

In the 1950 TT the experienced Ken Bills finished a highly creditable 12th in the Senior race on a Grey Flash at 83.79 mph. Not only this but George Brown and the young John Surtees put in some excellent performances on the 500 Vincent singles at British short circuits.

Surtees began racing in 1950 acquiring his Grey Flash at the end of that year. As an apprentice at one of the Vincent factories he was able to purchase an incomplete machine at a special price. He rode the machine until 1952, then home-prepared Manx Nortons, before becoming first a works rider for Norton and later the MV Agusta team leader and multi-world champion. His father Jack, a well-known racer in his own right, also campaigned a Vincent V-twin sidecar outfit with considerable success.

The standard Grey Flash was capable of around 110 mph, but the machines used by Surtees and Brown were both good for an extra 10 mph.

Unknown to many, the years 1949–51 were ones of considerable problems for the Vincent management as during June 1949 the company had gone into liquidation. However, under a receiver/manager it continued to trade and eventually in July 1952 Vincent's fortunes had picked up to the point where it was able to discharge the receiver and revert to normal trading conditions.

It was then able to survive until another spate of financial difficulties hit three years later in 1955, but this time the problems proved terminal.

Above
*Black Lightning engine details*

Overleaf
*The Surtees Vincent Equipe. Left to right : The Motor Cycle's Vic Willoughby and John Surtees discuss John's 499 cc Grey Flash, while John Mills and Surtees' father, Jack, stand with the latter's 998 cc racing outfit, 10 April 1952*

*Lance Capon thunders around Brands Hatch on his Vincent special, 1 August 1970. This combination was a potent force in British short-circuit events until a fatal accident deprived the sport of a truly colourful entry*

*The Swiss engineer Fritz Egli sprang to worldwide fame with his updated Vincent V-twin. This photograph dates from October 1967*

After the demise of the company many enthusiasts continued to keep the name in the headlines, but none more so than George Brown who became king of the dragstrip with a succession of record-breaking performances on machines such as *Nero* and *Super Nero*.

Later still, the Swiss engineer Fritz Egli designed a special frame to take the Vincent V-twin engine, and the Egli-Vincent (which also used Italian racing components such as Ceriani forks and Campagnolo mechanically-operated disc brakes) had several successful outings against more modern machines in the late 1960s. Incidentally the British Egli agent was none other than Roger Slater, later to become more well known for his Laverda activities.

Finally, mention should be made of Rae MacKay and Lance Capon who continued to campaign Vincent twins long after everyone else had called it a day. Both put on some truly superb performances which were sadly marred when Lance Capon suffered a fatal crash one day in the early 1970s at Brands Hatch, finally bringing the curtain down on the era of the thundering Stevenage V-twin as a competitive racing machine.

# 13
# Thruxton

This chapter sets out to chart the history of the long-distance Thruxton races for (standard!) production machines, events which played a significant role in the stories of many of the bikes described in this book.

The first such event was held on Saturday 25 June 1955 over the 2.76-mile Thruxton Airfield circuit in rural Hampshire. The rules stated that two riders for each machine would be allowed and the winning team would be the one which had completed the

*Typical Thruxton action. Triumph Tiger 110-mounted Frank Perris follows a couple of BSA Gold Star riders through a chicane at the inaugural event—then called the 'Nine Hour', 25 June 1955*

most laps on the ninth hour. No one rider was permitted to take over for more than two hours at a stretch.

Originally the event's organizers—the Ashton Combine—had envisaged a 24-hour or a 12-hour race, part of which would be run in darkness. However, they finally decided that for the first venture, at any rate, nine hours would be sufficient.

As things transpired, for most of the competitors nine hours was just about long enough. And amazingly the real problem which showed up was not rider fatigue or mechanical failure but tyres. The surface at Thruxton in those days was coarse so that tyre abrasion on corners was considerable. Front tyres suffered more than rear ones, and some of the

*A Norton Dominator receives attention during the 1955 Thruxton Nine Hour race*

harder riders were finding canvas showing before half distance! This situation was soon to cause a state of near panic as very few had come prepared with spare tyres or better still, spare wheels and tyres. Countless SOS calls were relayed over the public address system. Helpers and spectators lent tyres from their roadsters, whilst mechanics were sent scurrying to scour nearby Andover.

Although the meeting received a considerable amount of press coverage and was held under a national permit, few 'star' riders actually entered. Of the 45 teams whose entries had been accepted 43 came to the line for the start at noon.

Favourites were Eddie Dow and Eddie Crooks with a 499 cc BSA Gold Star. Others in contention were the Perris/Williams Triumph Tiger 110 and James/Lloyd 350 Gold Star. Other 'name' riders included Ron Langston and Derek Powell, whilst Syd Lawton first displayed his talents as a team manager by some efficient pit work.

At the end of the nine hours it was the Dow/Crooks Gold Star which crossed the line with the most laps (221) completed, second came James/Lloyd and third Williams/Shekell with a 498 cc Triumph Tiger 100.

The Perris/Williams Tiger 110 had led for a considerable section of the race but first an accident and then slipped timing put paid to their challenge. There were a total of 14 retirements for various reasons.

A year later, now organized by the Southampton Club, the Thruxton Marathon, as it was called in those days, was a much bigger affair with several well-known competitors among its 60 team entry.

Above right
*June 1955. Eddie Crooks (partnered by Eddie Dow) proved a race winner with this 499 cc BSA Gold Star*

Right
*Thruxton Nine Hour, 1955. The winning team—Dow (with glasses) and Crooks—looks happy at the finish*

Overleaf
*Tommy Morris, 350 BSA (5), and Michael Mintey, 350 Norton International (16), Thruxton 1957*

However, this didn't stop a major upset when the event was won by a 350, with the Ken James and Ivor Lloyd DB32 Gold Star completing 651 miles at an average speed of 72.3 mph. Even though there were also machines from Triumph, Norton, Royal Enfield and Velocette, BSA Gold Stars dominated the race taking the first six places overall. The entry included riders of the calibre of Bob McIntyre, Alastair King, Geoff Tanner, Roy Ingram, Tony Godfrey, Eddie Crooks, Bernard Codd, Percy Tait and Rex Avery. So the James/Lloyd victory was an exceptional performance in more than one respect.

If anyone had placed bets that a 350 wouldn't win again they were to be proved wrong when Rex Avery and Fred Webber took their Gold Star to victory in the 1957 event. But for over 500 miles Ken James, now with Ed Minihan as co-rider, led the race yet again only to have his engine lock up when the crankpin seized.

The Avery/Webber machine had in fact finished the 1956 event in third spot and since then covered 12,000 road miles, with only new valves and springs fitted during the entire period. This illustrates some-

**Above**
*Thruxton Nine Hour, 1957. At the sixth-hour pitstop. Cyril Hallburn of BSA checks the plug on the Eckart-Wallis Gold Star, then in the lead. Later, it retired with magneto trouble*

**Above right**
*Dan Shorey, mechanic, Mike Hailwood and Stan Hailwood after winning the 1958 Thruxton marathon aboard a Triumph T110*

**Right**
*Tony Godfrey in action during the 1959 event. Machine is the newly-introduced twin-carburettor Triumph T120 Bonneville*

thing of the reliability factor of this particular machine. Unlike the previous year, the 1957 Thruxton Nine Hours saw a 649 cc Triumph Tiger 110 finish second and a 692 cc Royal Enfield Super Meteor come home third. The latter machine was without doubt the fastest bike in the race but vibration caused problems including a split tank. The

event saw a high retirement rate—out of 43 starters 23 went out, 19 of these attributed to machine failure. Some blamed the weather, which after all was the hottest in 10 years. *The Motor Cycle* race report headline read: 'Freak weather and freak happenings'.

Then in 1958 the name was changed to the Thruxton 500-Mile Race, and the event was witnessing new levels of interest from both spectators and manufacturers. Not only this, but for the first time a multi-cylinder machine took the chequered flag, in the shape of a Triumph Tiger 110 ridden by Dan Shorey and the fast maturing young star, Mike Hailwood.

The pairing of Shorey and Hailwood completed 220 laps in 7 hours 35 minutes, with an average speed of 66 mph. The 1000 cc singles category went to an International Norton whilst a BSA Gold Star took the 350 cc honours.

For the first time none of the top six finishers overall was mounted on a Gold Star and all were twins: Triumph first and fifth, Royal Enfield second and third, Norton sixth and the first foreign entry, a 595 cc BMW R69, which came home fourth. But the duel for the lead was fought out between the Triumph of Shorey/Hailwood and the Bob McIntyre/Derek Powell Royal Enfield Super Meteor, with a lap separating them at the finish.

The 1959 event saw a BMW R69 take victory. Initial leaders McIntyre and Eric Hinton's bid came to an end after the primary chaincase shed its oil, the chain broke and after repairs, McIntyre subsequently spilled at the Anchor Corner chicane which signalled the team's retirement. The lead then went to the Triumph Bonneville (new that year) of Tony Godfrey and Brian Holder, but seven minutes at their pit at the 350-mile stage to fix a loose dynamo cost them the race.

BSA Gold Stars won both the 1000 cc single-cylinder and 350 cc classes, whilst an NSU made it two German wins by taking the newly-introduced 250 cc category. *The Motor Cycle* reported: 'This year's 500-miler was the best in the series and was attended by a record crowd and held in brilliant weather'.

The foreign challenge was curbed the following year when all four categories—General (overall), Multi-cylinder (over 500 cc), Senior (350–500 cc)

*Phil Read (on bike) and Brian Setchell with the Norton 650SS on which they won both the 1962 and 1963 Thruxton 500-mile races. Photograph is from the 1962 event*

and Lightweight (250 cc)—were won by British bikes. Ron Langston and Don Chapman took their 646 cc AJS 31 CSR to both the General and the Multi-cylinder class victories. A Norton Dominator piloted by Fred Swift and Dennis Greenfield won the Senior, whilst the Lightweight went to the Syd Lawton-entered Royal Enfield Crusader Sports of Ray Prowting and Mike Munday.

By now the event was a most closely fought contest with *works* machines making their bow through the leading dealers in the land. The performances of the machines concerned were publicized by the press and in the manufacturers' own brochures. A win at Thruxton was by now a major weapon for sales . . . and would be even more important as sales declined over the next few years.

The first time two long-distance events were held in Britain was in 1961 as the Thruxton marathon was joined by the BMCRC (British Motor Cycle Racing Club) 1000 Kilometres at Silverstone. But Thruxton continued in its number one role (the rival 1000-kilometre event only lasted two years). At the Hampshire venue the Senior class went once again to the Norton pair of Swift and Greenfield whilst, horror upon horror, a Japanese Honda took the Lightweight honours. But at least British bike fans could take heart from the fact that overall victory went to the Alec Bennett-entered Triumph Bonneville ridden by Tony Godfrey and John Holder. Surprisingly, the 497 cc Norton 88 of Swift and Greenfield was second overall and Tom Thorpe and Roy Mayhew on a Velocette Venom third, these half-litre models finishing in front of many larger capacity twins. for the second year running the Ariel Arrows just missed out on winning the 250 cc category.

Stars abounded—even if they didn't do the winning with names such as Bob McIntyre, Alastair King, John Hartle, Phil Read, Sammy Miller, Cecil Sandford and former World Speedway Champion Tommy Price, to name but a few.

The beginning of a famous combination—that of Phil Read and Brian Setchell on Syd Lawton's Norton 650SS was witnessed in 1962. Quite simply it just cleared off at the start and won by seven laps from Roy Ingram and Fred Swift on another Norton, this time the smaller 88. Whilst in the Lightweight (250 cc) class yet again an Ariel Arrow finished second for the third year running, with a Honda taking the glory. Another problem was the track surface, which by now was beginning to crack up badly. One must remember that Thruxton was still only an old wartime airfield with straw bales to mark the course—not a pukka purpose-built race circuit as it is today.

*The Motor Cycle* in their 28 June 1962 issue, summed up the Thruxton 500 miles perfectly; 'Skill and pluck, excitement, panic and frustration. You find them all at Thruxton's annual marathon. If you relish the full, rich flavour of race enthusiasm—with top stars, rabbits and all grades between dicing for the sheer love of it—you can't afford to miss it.'

If the results of the 1963 Silverstone 1000 kilometres were anything to go by then that year's Thruxton 500-miler would have been dominated by the Tom Kirby-entered Matchless 650 CSR of Paddy Driver and Joe Dunphy, but a stone thrown up from the crumbling Thruxton tarmac fetched off the spring link of the rear chain whilst they were leading during the first hour. So victory went for the second time to the Lawton-entered 650SS of Read and Setchell, with the Triumph Bonneville of Syd Mizen/John Holder second and another Meriden big twin third. Then came an AJS 650 CSR, the Triumph T100SS of 500 cc class winners Davis/Scott and in sixth place the Geoff Dodkin-entered Velocette Venom of Phillips/Thorp.

The 250 cc category was an extremely closely contributed affair with a works 196 cc Bultaco only 1 minute 25 seconds ahead of the Scuderia Duke Royal Enfield Crusader Super 5 of Hartle/Buxton.

The next year, 1964, saw the tenth Thruxton marathon which happened to be the last for a number of years. So perhaps it was fitting that not only should Brian Setchell (with stand-in rider Derek Woodman) and Syd Lawton's Norton win once again, but a British bike should gain victory in the 250 cc class. The latter machine was an AJS 14 CSR. Ridden by Peter Williams and Tony Wood it pulled off perhaps the biggest surprise of the whole series by defeating the large entry which was predominantly foreign. Entries included Japanese Honda and Yamaha, Spanish Montesa and Italian Ducati machinery.

The following year, 1965, saw the by now famous event moved from Thruxton to Castle Coombe. Quite simply this was necessary because the years of racing combined with neglect had wreaked havoc on the Thruxton tarmac surface. The 500-miler did not return to its original home for several years, being staged first at Castle Coombe and then at Brands Hatch. Somehow the later events were not quite the same—the change of venue and the growing Japanese dominance saw to that.

Today, as one of those lucky enough to have witnessed the titanic battles during the late 1950s and early 1960s at Thruxton Airfield, I can only hope to have recorded what is without doubt an important segment in the history of British racing during the so-called classic era.

*Riders sprint across the crumbling Thruxton tarmac to get the 1960 500-miler under way*

# Index